JIM EARLY'S

Reflections

THE MEMORIES AND RECIPES OF A SOUTHERN COOK

Published by The Best Tar Heel Barbecue Manteo to Murphy, Inc.
http://www.jimearly.com

Jim Early's Reflections: The Memories and Recipes of a Southern Cook
ISBN: 0-9722979-1-X

Library of Congress Control Number: 2005905509

Suggested Retail Price: $34.95 plus tax

Cover and Book Design:
Steve McCulloch
Raleigh, NC

Food Photography:
Peter Christopher Hutson
PCH Photography
Raleigh, NC

Photo of Author for Cover and Foreword:
Lloyd Aaron Photography
Winston-Salem, NC

Printed by Harperprints
One Industry Drive
Henderson, NC 27536
1-800-682-5948

Manufactured in the United States of America

First Printing 2005

I dedicate this book to all the great Southern cooks (past and present) who have lovingly labored with stooped shoulders and gnarled hands – black, brown and white – to provide their family and friends with a gift of love and to Southern chefs resplendent in their whites who have brought and continue to bring magic to the kitchens of the South. I bow in sincere appreciation and acknowledgement of your time, talents and gifts that have placed, in my opinion, Southern cooking with those offerings that encompass the pinnacle of epicurean experiences.

ACKNOWLEDGEMENTS

*F*irst I wish to express my love and appreciation to my children –
Jim, Anna and Mary Elizabeth – for their continued support and
encouragement while I was writing this book. Each of them has served as
taste testers, proofreaders and marketing consultants. I have great repoire
with my children and their constructive criticism of some of my initial efforts, though given in love, was unvarnished. Thanks "guys."

I also wish to express my thanks and appreciation to the young woman
who manages my law office – Amanda Brooks. Amanda is not only my
office manager, paralegal, secretary and good right and left hand, but she
possesses interest and cooking skills far beyond her tender years due in no
small part to her Italian and Southern background. Thanks Amanda.

I would be remiss if I did not thank my friends at Knollwood Baptist
church, the Forsyth County Courthouse, the ladies at my local BB&T
branch, restaurant owners across the state and others who continued to
inquire about the progress of the book and served as taste testers for my
creations. Their encouragement, along with my children and staff sus-
tained me through twelve hour days, seven days a week for a period of approximately two years as I created the recipes and wrote this book. Thanks
to each of you.

Most of all I would like to thank the sponsor that has made the printing and the future printing of this book possible. My heart felt thanks to
Branch Banking & Trust Company (BB&T) and

FRIENDS OF FEED THE CHILDREN

TABLE OF CONTENTS

TABLE OF CONTENTS

$\mathcal{W}$hen our paths first crossed, Jim Early had just completed his first semester as a freshman at Wake Forest University and I had just completed my first semester as college dean. Jim was a bright young man and enthusiastic about everything he pursued. Unfortunately his studies did not rank high on that list. We had our "we need to talk" visit. He told me that he was the first child in his family to attend college and discussed the demands and difficulties of attending Wake Forest as

The author

a day student and living at home. He felt he needed a quiet atmosphere, conducive to study, and I suggested that he go to Mars Hill Junior College: advice that he accepted. He returned to Wake Forest after a couple of years, completed his Bachelor of Arts degree, and went on immediately for a Juris Doctor degree from our School of Law.

A number of years have passed since Jim finished his program at Wake Forest. Jim and I have remained friends, and he continues to be a successful trial lawyer here in Winston-Salem. Areas of special concern to him are personal injury, malpractice, employment claims, and family law, and, among his other legal experiences, he was trial attorney in landmark cases on Covenants Not to Compete for Doctors in North Carolina. He is also a certified Superior Court mediator.

Jim is an active churchman – a sometime deacon and Sunday School teacher – and he is the father of three children, two daughters and one son, for whom he has an obvious and deep love. So it is not surprising that the tactics and techniques of an attorney's career matter less to him than the various human and ethical considerations that are – or should be – central to a lawyer's life. He is a frequent and effective speaker on such subjects as "Ethics: More than a Line in the Sand" and "Seven Steps to Balance." He likes to say that his public appearances are about the "quality of life," and he has spoken not only to fellow lawyers as a participant in the CLE (Continuing Legal Education) program of the North Carolina Bar Association but also to gatherings as far away as New Mexico and South Dakota.

Beyond his law office and even beyond the audiences to whom he speaks, Jim seeks opportunities to help people in need. For example, in September 1999, when Hurricane Floyd hit eastern North Carolina with devastating force, Jim spent a week working side by side with the Army National Guard: recovering 181 corpses washed from their graves at Princeville, offering stress management seminars to his co-workers, and contributing his own funds and clothes to people who had "lost everything." Other disasters, hurricanes and tornados have come to North Carolina and Jim has volunteered to be there, doing whatever might be possible to bring encouragement and relief.

It would be a mistake, however, to conclude that Jim Early's life is all working and doing good deeds for others. He also likes to hunt and fish, to ride horses and breed bird dogs, to fly planes, to play in bands, and to dance. And – more to the point – he writes books. And – at least of equal importance – he cooks, he knows food of all types and varieties, and he writes about cooking with knowledge and with passion.

Here in Winston-Salem Jim has offered cooking courses at Salem College. The title of one of his classes was "The World's Best Brunswick Stew"; another was called "The Best Tarheel Barbecue from Manteo to Murphy." For those who were not present for his classes, we can capture his recipes and his style – and his taste – by reading his 2002 book which carries the same title as his Salem lecture: *The Best Tarheel Barbecue Manteo to Murphy*. Buy a copy, keep it in your car, and look at it whenever you are going across North Carolina from east to west or from north to south. You will be richly rewarded.

And now, as another episode in his crowded and amazingly versatile life, we have *Jim Early's Reflections: The Memories and Recipes of a Southern Cook*. I wish that I were a qualified cook myself so that as an "expert" I could tell you how good it is. But I am not a cook and only have memories of food that others have cooked: my mother's chicken salad and my neighbor Mrs. Fagge's fried apple pies and my Aunt Lottie's "boiled custard" and Miss Mattie Bassett's "hot biscuits" and my sister Elizabeth's caramel cake: all of them, like Jim Early, "Southerners." And in recent weeks I have had barbecue in three of the restaurants that Jim has recommended, and I know that his judgment is sound.

But the best thing to do is to read his recipes and, if you can't cook yourself, ask somebody else to try them. As for me, I'll be looking for someone, maybe my wife or one of my two daughters, to prepare some "red deviled eggs" or that "shrimp, artichoke and pistachio nut dip" or the "blue cheese, grapes and toasted almond dip" or the "Bartlett pear, Stilton cheese and toasted hazelnut dip" or, for dessert, a "'killer" coconut pie. And there would still be thirty five recipes left. There is much to look forward to.

Who would have thought that the eighteen-year-old boy I met many years ago would become not only a lawyer and speaker and ethicist and citizen volunteer but also such a hugely talented and creative cook? And yet Jim Early's history tells us that the story is true.

Edwin G. Wilson
Provost Emeritus
Wake Forest University

INTRODUCTION

*T*he South is different. I would not tout that it is better than the North, Midwest or West coast. It is simply, wonderfully different. The South has a different history – some of it good, some of it not so good. I hope that we have moved beyond those issues that were not so good for so many. I hope that we have come to a time and a place that we can recognize the contributions, the gifts, the time and the talents of all who made and continue to make the South a special place.

The South appeals to all of my senses. The South appeals to my eyes. I am intrigued by visions of quiet lanes, meandering through stately live oaks with veils of Spanish moss, pecan groves, snowy fields of cotton encircled by long needled pines, languid harbors with gently rocking shrimp boats, smoky haze over the soft curves of her mountains, palmetto palms, blue water and white sugary beaches.

My soul embraces the sounds of the South. I enjoy the melancholy, plaintive sounds of the blues. My heart skips when a jazz sideman takes a ride, my toes tap to the funky zydeco of a Cajun band, my spirits rise with the boogie of gulf coast jump and I cannot stay in my seat when they are cranking out a good Texas two step or shag music at the beach.

The South quickens my sense of smell. A gentle morning breeze moves across a Texas prairie bearing the slightly acrid sent of sage. The warmth of first light stirs the air that moves the fog amidst the gray cypress ghosts and carries the faint smell of cinnamon across the indigo waters of the bayou. Southern breezes transmit the sweet sent of oranges to the traveler on the interstate. Commercial cleaners try but cannot reproduce the fresh clean smell of a forest of long leaf pines. No bottled fragrance will ever capture the smell of gardenias wafting across a porch on a soft summer night.

I seek the touch of things Southern. My journey has permitted me to pick cotton, prime tobacco, work on fishing boats and learn a bit about logging. They each have different textures and touches. It pleases my sense of touch to shuck oysters, peel shrimp, detail crayfish, shuck corn, string beans and hull peas. I enjoy picking tomatoes, oranges, peaches and apples in season. I welcome the incredibly soft feel of a newborn calf or lamb. To hold the rich black loamy soil of eastern North Carolina in my hand gives me pleasure.

Of all my senses the greatest beneficiary of my life in the South has been and continues to be my sense of taste. When it comes to ranking the great food areas of the country, the South, in my opinion, is without peer. I have been privileged to eat in a number of fine restaurants, mom and pop cafés and private homes in Alaska and the contiguous lower 48 states. I have eaten in restaurants and homes in a number of foreign countries. I have yet to find an area that places as much emphasis on good food and fellowship as the South. Be it briskets, jambalaya, catfish, crab, oysters, quail, barbecue or country ham – there are few areas of the South that do not produce fantastic table fare. This is due in no small part to the fact that Southerners associate food and celebration. It is my opinion that Southerners enjoy life more than any other group of people in the country. Because some areas are sparsely populated, dining becomes the hub of social life in many small towns. Folks in eastern North Carolina do not give a second thought to driving 50 or 60 miles to check out a new restaurant or barbecue place.

It has been my observation that most women throughout the world love and nurture through the stomach. Nowhere is this more true than in the South. For generations Southern wives and mothers have taken great delight in preparing a special meal or dish to say I love you. This form of embrace carries over to community as well. If there is an illness or death, Southern women bring their signature offering to the sick or the bereaved family of the deceased. It expresses caring and a wish to comfort. Eating in celebration can take the form of family reunions, wedding rehearsals, parties, holidays and birthdays, down to the most simple of events such as "Have you had a good day?" "You have?" "Well honey lets cook a pig or make a stew or turn a freezer of cream or go out to supper." While this emphasis on food may be perplexing to those from other areas of the country, to those reared in the South it makes perfect sense.

I have had the good fortune to be reared in a family of outstanding Southern country cooks. The great ladies of the Hicks' clan (my mother's family) including my mother, Aunt Pearl, Mama Hicks (my maternal grandmother), Aunt Irma, Aunt Madie, Pat, Leigh and a host of other good Southern cooks across the South have graciously shared their knowledge, skills and stories with me since I was four years of age. Some of my friends say I have an "old soul." This may well be, and if so I am proud of it. The knowledge and stories shared by these women have played a major role in shaping not only my interest in cooking, but the core values I possess and the man I became.

The two major male role models in my life, my dad and Papa Hicks (my maternal grandfather), also contributed to my interest in food and my core values, morals and ethics. My dad's forte was grilling. He took great delight in cooking for the men that worked for his trucking company. I remember helping him with fish frys and chicken frys and feeding several hundred men supper at the neighborhood park.

I don't recall ever seeing Papa Hicks cook anything or even make a pot of coffee. My recollection is that Mama Hicks did all the cooking of every sort and "spoiled him rotten." I remember that her place at the table placed her within reach of the oven and that she took hot biscuits from the oven for Papa Hicks as he finished the one before him. Few men had life so good as I recall his. Though he did not prepare it, Papa Hicks was a stickler for trying to obtain the best and freshest food available in eastern North Carolina. To that end I think he succeeded admirably. He did not teach me how to cook, but he certainly contributed to my taste and appreciation of good food and fellowship. He also shared his "old school" ideas of what constitutes a Southern gentleman and a sportsman. For these lessons I am eternally grateful.

In the summer of 2003 Southern Foodways Alliance of Oxford Mississippi held a pimento cheese contest open to all of its members, foodies and followers. I am advised that there were more than 300 entries from across the country for the contest.

In the course of teaching gourmet cooking classes at Salem College in Winston-Salem, North Carolina and writing the book *Shining Times: The Adventures and Recipes of a Sportsman,* I had developed dozens of original recipes. I had never however, entered any of my cooking creations in a contest. With the encouragement of friends I decided to enter Southern Foodways Alliance's pimento cheese contest. Using my mother's simple country pimento cheese recipe as a baseline, I set about to create the best pimento cheese I could imagine. When I was satisfied with my efforts I entered my recipe in the Southern Foodways Alliance contest along with the story that appears in this book.

To my delight, a month or so after entering the contest I received a call from John T. Edge, Director of Southern Foodways Alliance. John T. advised that out of all the entries in the pimento cheese contest, my pimento cheese recipe had been voted one of the top three entries. I was pleased with this news and shared it with a friend of mine who owns one of the top restaurants in town. He decided the recipe needed to be put on his menu as an appetizer. He did this and I supplied the restaurant with the dip for several months. The dip was so well received that he requested that I create other dips in keeping with the season. It was then October. I returned to my kitchen and created pumpkin and sweet potato dips. These dips and others were well received and fused the desire to create more dips and write this book.

In the preparation of this book I had three goals: (1) To recapture Old South memories from those kinder and gentler times when I was a child in eastern North Carolina and from my travels across the South as an adult. (2) To share some of the great food dishes that I associated with those memories. (3) To take these scrumptious dishes to a new level and present them in the form of dips and spreads that could be enjoyed by a number of people so that all who shared the offering could experience a unique taste that captured Old South memories with a New South twist.

Bookshelves are replete with recipes for dips and desserts. Most of the dip and spread recipes that I have read seem to have as a goal, dumping some ingredients together and creating a quick dip that was reasonably good and would serve a need. It was never my goal to create such a dip. In these dips I wanted to create something so very special that the person served would know that the host had gone the extra mile to create an offering that not only excited the palate, but spoke, "You are my special friend."

Some of these dips have a list of ingredients that would be taxing to prepare all of the various ingredients just to make the dip. For those dips you may wish to create a meal that incorporates the ingredients on a night prior to your party saving requisite amounts of the ingredients for your dip the following day. Thus you, your family and friends can share the meal that is part of the memories and also produce the ingredients for your dip and reduce your preparation time on your busy day.

The desserts in this book were not included to simply provide the reader with another dessert recipe. The desserts in this book are some of the very best that I have been able to find in my travels across the South improved to the best of my abilities and skills. They are my favorites. I hope they become yours.

It is my fond wish that each reader enjoy the stories that accompany the recipes in this book and perhaps one or more stories will rekindle memories of their childhood or stories of childhoods shared by their parents. If some of these recipes and stories take you to a special place, then my goal has been met and my journey complete. Bon appètit.

Jim Early

SECTION 1

Country Cooking Dips and Spreads

As a child I lived inside the city limits of a small eastern North Carolina town. One could hardly call our family "city folks" as our neighbor two houses up owned and kept a cow and to my delight often a pony or two. My mother's family (the Hicks) settled and lived at Hicks' Crossroads about ten miles from town. All of the Hicks' family had farm animals. My Aunt Pearl, the matriarch of the Hicks' clan, perhaps having the most unusual of Old Macdonald's creatures. Aunt Pearl had a number of chickens. The one I remember most vividly was "Red." Red was a Rhode Island Red hen that looked like Big Bird x 10. Red and Aunt Pearl had an understanding. Aunt Pearl would not arrange a meeting between Red and the Sunday dinner table and Red agreed not to eat Aunt Pearl like a cricket when she gathered eggs. Uncle Willie (Aunt Pearl's husband) never made peace with Red and he generally carried a stick of wood or a sidearm in his hand when he crossed the yard.

Red was not only big but she crowed. The barnyard rooster quickly learned that despite his inch and a half spurs, that if Red wanted to crow it was best to let her do her thing. In fact mules, pigs and junkyard dogs all found other things to do when Red made her rounds and if Red was having a bad hair day the whole community stayed indoors.

Now Red never laid many eggs, apparently not thinking it was worth her while or in her job description, but when she did, as Aunt Pearl was fond of saying, "Lord child it was a doosey." I don't know how much Red's eggs weighed but I took a picture of one and the negative weighed five pounds. One of Red's eggs hard boiled in the vat used for scalding hogs and sliced with a cross cut saw could produce more deviled egg than the Hicks clan could eat at a family reunion followed by an all day church meeting with dinner on the grounds.

Uncle Willie and Aunt Pearl passed some years ago. Red, 59 years young and a spinster left too. She simply vanished. No one in Vance

County has seen Red in ten years. However, there are reports drifting out of the bayou country of a big red bird that stalks the swamps pecking at alligators, fishing boats and low flying planes. Is it Red? I'd bet the farm. And those Cajun folk who think they found dinosaur droppings on a small island in the Delta need to be looking for an egg. It's time for the Hicks' reunion and those good folk could be missing out on some fine eatin – Red Deviled Eggs Cajun style.

The following is my version of Aunt Pearl's Red Deviled Eggs recipe I found written on a Sears & Roebuck order blank. I have done the conversions, interpolations and converted country to Cajun. Enjoy!

---

12 eggs
10 ounces sharp white cheddar cheese
4 ounces cream cheese
¼ cup chopped green bell peppers (Rice Crispy-sized pieces)
¼ cup chopped red bell peppers (Rice Crispy-sized pieces)
⅓ cup sweet pickle cubes
8 tablespoons mayonnaise
4 tablespoons jarred pimento slices (drained)
2 tablespoons ground hot red peppers
⅓ cup jarred jalapeño slices chopped medium-fine (drained)
¼ cup chopped green onions (Rice Crispy-sized pieces)
1 tablespoon worcestershire sauce
Two 2.8 ounce packages Oscar Meyer Real Bacon Recipe brand bacon pieces
1 cup roasted salted peanuts
8 teaspoons Louisiana brand hot sauce
3 pinch spoons of Tony Chachere's Original Creole Seasoning

Hard boil eggs. To hard boil eggs I simply place eggs on their side in a single layer in a sauce pan and cover the eggs with water by approximately ½ inch. Do not stand the eggs on end to gain more space. To do so will cause the yoke to droop to the bottom end of the egg and your cup will not be centered if you slice your eggs lengthwise. Bring water to a boil, cover, reduce heat to medium and cook for approximately 12 minutes. Drain hot water from sauce pan and replace with cold tap water. Let eggs rest for a minute or so until they are cool enough to handle. Crack egg gently on edge of sauce pan and peel carefully under cold running tap water. I start my peel at the large end of the egg. Once you have broken the membrane you can slide the membrane and shell easily with your thumb, turning the egg from the smaller end with your other hand.

While eggs are boiling, in a food processor grate white cheddar cheese. Remove grated cheese from food processor and insert chopping blade. Replace grated cheese in food processor and add cream cheese in pinch-sized pieces. Add chopped bell peppers, sweet pickle cubes and mayonnaise to mixture. Add pimento slices, jalapeños and ground hot red pepper to mixture. Add chopped green onions and worcestershire sauce to mixture. Turn mixture in processor with a fork so that some of the more moist ingredients and the mayonnaise are at the bottom of the processor. Blend mixture checking every 15 seconds for approximately 30-45 seconds. You should have a pimento cheese type consistency.

Slice the boiled and peeled eggs lengthwise, not across. Turn the eggs face down toward a bowl and press gently with your forefinger and the yolk will usually pop out. If it does not, gently scoop the yolk out with a wet teaspoon. Place yolks in medium-sized mixing bowl. Place egg white halves on a large tray for stuffing. Mash egg yolks with fork until the yolks are M&M-sized pieces. 12 yolks make 2 cups of chopped egg yolk.

Remove cheese mixture to medium-sized mixing bowl. Warm bacon pieces in a frying pan for 3 minutes. Add bacon to cheese mixture. Chop peanuts to medium-sized pieces (Rice Crispy size) and add nuts to cheese mixture. Fold with rubber spatula. Add hot sauce and creole seasoning to cheese mixture. Fold with a rubber spatula. Add 2 cups cheese mixture to egg yolks. Fold cheese mixture and chopped egg yolks gently with a fork. Do not over-fold as you do not wish the egg yolks to get lost in the cheese mixture. With a tablespoon fill the hard boiled egg half cavities with your mixture. Fill the egg halves carefully to keep them as clean and white as possible. If you need to clean an egg white use a paper towel and cold water to blot any excess that detracts from your offering. Total preparation time is approximately 1 hour.

This recipe makes about 2 pounds. This is enough stuffing for 48 egg halves with approximately 2 cups left over. Serve the leftover stuffing on water crackers.

BLACK-EYED PEAS, HAM HOCK, PEPPERS AND MEXICAN CORN DIP

$\mathcal{F}$rom birth to school age I had the privilege to live next door to my mother's parents in the little eastern North Carolina town of Henderson. My maternal grandparents were known in the community as Joe and Cora Hicks. To me they were Papa and Mama Hicks. I adored them. Papa Hicks' signature gift was to cut gardenia blooms off of the huge bushes around their house and layer them in shoe boxes with wax paper to be delivered to the ladies at McCracken Oil Company. All the ladies had brandy snifters to float their gardenia blooms. Mama Hicks taught the seventeen year old girls Sunday school class at First Baptist Church for at least three hundred years. She also cut the edges from Merita White Bread and toasted the centers for the communion squares on communion Sunday.

Mama Hicks was one of those wonderful Southern cooks who made every dish from recipes learned at her mother's side; her mother acquired her knowledge in the same fashion. Mama Hicks never measured anything. It had to coat a spoon, drip "right," roll into a ball that felt right, etc. She did not wear a watch and did not have a kitchen clock but got her time of day from the radio she played for company. She seemed to intuitively know when to open the oven and remove her treasures. She rarely peeked.

Joe & Cora Hicks

During the week my father was away in Winston-Salem helping Malcolm McLean and his family birth McLean Trucking Company. While Dad was away, Mother and I ate most of our suppers with Papa and Mama Hicks. Mama Hicks cooked Old South and country offerings. Few meals are more indigenous to the South than Mama Hicks' presentation of a big pot of black-eyed peas cooked with ham hock, collard greens, country ham, deviled eggs and crackling corn bread. This feast is usually enjoyed with sweet tea or buttermilk. This recipe is a typical Old South country supper. People in the country ate breakfast, dinner (the noon time meal) and supper. They did not "do lunch."

15.8 ounce can Bush's brand black-eyed peas cooked with ham hock
4 biscuit-sized slices of country ham (makes 1 cup cooked ham)
$\frac{1}{3}$ of whole green pepper chopped medium-fine
$\frac{1}{3}$ of whole red pepper chopped medium-fine
$\frac{1}{2}$ cup yellow corn (frozen is fine)
8 ounces sharp white cheddar cheese
4 ounces cream cheese
4 heaping tablespoons sour cream
2 heaping tablespoons mayonnaise
2 pinches salt
1 tablespoon worcestershire sauce
4 teaspoons Texas Pete brand hot sauce
1 tablespoon chopped onion
$\frac{1}{4}$ stick salted butter
1 pinch black pepper

Heat can of black-eyed peas with ham hock in medium saucepan per directions on can, drain and toss liquid. Cook country ham per *Tips for Cooking* section at the end of this book. Pour ham juices over peas. Cook yellow corn with butter, a pinch of salt and a pinch of black pepper.

Grate white cheddar cheese in food processor. Remove grated cheese from food processor and insert chopping blade. Replace grated cheese in food processor and add cream cheese in pinches, add sour cream, worcestershire sauce, mayonnaise, a pinch of salt, Texas Pete and onion. Blend cheeses and spices in food processor checking every 15 seconds until you achieve a smooth creamy dip consistency (about 30-45 seconds) that will hold on a cracker or rigid chip. Remove to mixing bowl.

Coarse chop peas (lightly buzz). Remove all fat (if any) from country ham and any stringy fibers. Tear ham or cut into small pieces about the size of half of a dime by hand or by buzzing in food processor.

Add peas, ham, peppers and corn to the cheese blend and gently fold with whisk. Total preparation time is approximately 2 hours.

Makes 40 ounces. Serve on corn sticks or corn flavored tortilla chips.

COLLARD, COUNTRY HAM, DEVILED EGG
AND ROASTED PEPPERS DIP

As previously shared in the preamble to the Black-Eyed Pea recipe, as a very young boy I grew up in an eastern North Carolina town living next door to my mother's parents Joe and Cora Hicks. Papa Hicks worked for McCracken Oil Company and called on all the farmers in Vance County and the three surrounding counties for their fuel/oil needs to heat their homes and cure tobacco if they did not use wood for these purposes. From age four I went to bed at 7:00 p.m. so I could get up at 4:30 a.m. and have breakfast with Papa and Mama Hicks. I then accompanied Papa Hicks on his rounds. Papa Hicks was a company man to a fault. He always gave the company its dues. He just decided to do this between 6:00 a.m. and 3:00 p.m. instead of 8:00 a.m. and 5:00 p.m. During hunting season Papa Hicks carried his favorite bird dog (an English Setter named Ted) in the trunk of his car filled with hay and properly ventilated by wooden blocks to prevent the lid from closing. I in turn had a palate on the back seat for "naps."

At 5:00 a.m. I was dressed in my brown canvas hunting clothes, boots, gloves and watchcap and ready for breakfast. Mama Hicks always provided me with a small cup of coffee with lots of cream so Papa Hicks and I could sip coffee together. Papa Hicks would only drink Luzianne coffee with chicory or Pilot Knob. Thus at an early age I had an acquired taste for strong coffee. As Papa Hicks had a fondness for saying, "It doesn't take a whole lot of water to make good coffee."

At 5:30 a.m. we were on the road. At 6:00 a.m. we were in some farmer's cow parlor as he visited and did the renewal for the fuel/oil. Sometimes I got to help the farmer milk the cow (many stories here).

Between farms I absorbed Papa Hicks' wisdom and take on life. Some friends say I have an "old soul." If this is true it is due in no small part to the stories I heard at my Aunt Pearl's knee and the time spent traveling with Papa Hicks. A mini nap on my pallet around 10:00 a.m. and this young hunter was ready for lunch at a country store at 11:00 a.m. This meal usually consisted of a can of salmon opened with the liqueur poured off and some vinegar added, eaten with saltine crackers or sardines pre-pared much the same or a bologna sandwich sliced to order with mustard and white bread, all washed down with RC Colas and dessert was sharing a Moonpie.

At 3:00 p.m. Papa Hicks concluded his work day on a farm that had been carefully chosen when he had planned his route that morning. A brief pause for Papa Hicks to slip off his Johnny Bull shoes and pull his brown canvas hunting clothes on over his blue pinstriped suit, boot up and grab his old Remington Model 11 auto five was all that was required for him to be ready to bird hunt. Bird hunting or "burd hunting" in the South means quail hunting.

Papa Hicks and all the farmers he had called on for years were like family. The farmer on the farms where we hunted would always tell Papa Hicks how many coveys he had and where we should look at that time of day. Papa Hicks rarely missed a shot. A number of times he would wait for two birds to cross and take two with one shot. He never carried more than a half dozen shells and he never shot more than four or five birds for the table.

After a couple of hours hunting we loaded up and headed for home. We would arrive just after dark, feed and kennel Ted and wash up for one of Mama Hicks' great country suppers. One of her favorite meals was collard greens, country ham, deviled eggs, hot potato salad, corn pudding, stewed tomatoes and spoon bread. I have incorporated that meal into this dip and tickled it with a few condiments that enhance its flavor. This dip is Old South country cooking at its best. I hope you agree.

---

2 cups frozen collard greens thawed, destemmed and medium chopped
1 baseball-sized ham hock
4 slices biscuit-sized country ham ($^3/_4$ cup chopped country ham when cooked)
8 ounces sharp white cheddar cheese
4 ounces cream cheese
3 tablespoons jarred roasted red peppers (drained)
4 heaping tablespoons sour cream
1 tablespoon chopped onion
1 pickled egg (makes $^1/_4$ cup chopped egg)
$^1/_2$ cup salted peanuts, medium chop (i.e. $^1/_2$ original size)
2 heaping tablespoons mayonnaise
1 tablespoon worcestershire sauce
$^1/_2$ tablespoon yellow mustard
3 pinch spoons Texas Pete brand hot sauce
1 tablespoon crushed red pepper

Place collard greens and $^1/_3$ cup water with a baseball-sized ham hock, add crushed red pepper and cook for approximately 15 minutes over medium heat. Set aside covered. Cook country ham per *Tips for Cooking* section at the end of this book. Remove ham to plate and set aside. Add $^1/_4$ cup water to ham drippings and stir and scrape well. Pour over collards.

Grate white cheddar cheese in food processor. Remove grated cheese from food processor and insert chopping blade. Replace grated cheese in food processor and add cream cheese in teaspoon-sized pieces, add sour cream, roasted red peppers, chopped onions, mayonnaise, mustard, worcestershire sauce and Texas Pete. Blend in food processor checking every 15 seconds until you achieve a smooth creamy dip consistency (about 30-45 seconds) that will hold on a cracker or rigid chip. Pour the cheese mixture into a large mixing bowl.

Slice pickled egg into $^1/_4$ inch slices and place in clean food processor. Buzz until coarse chopped (about 4 or 5 seconds) and set aside. Remove all fat (if any) from country ham and any stringy fibers. Tear ham into small pieces about the size of half of a dime by hand or by buzzing in food processor. Add chopped egg, chopped peanuts, 1 cup chopped collard greens and chopped ham to the cheese mixture and gently fold the greens, eggs, ham and peanuts into the cheese mixture with a whisk. Total preparation time is approximately 1½ hours.

Makes 8 + cups. Serve on corn sticks or corn flavored tortilla chips.

CORN PUDDING SOUFFLÉ AND TOASTED PECAN DIP

*I*n my youth all special occasions celebrated by the Hicks' clan, including Thanksgiving, Christmas, Easter, birthdays, good hair days, etc., were celebrated at the Hicks' family home place and residence of my favorite aunt, Pearl Hicks Woody. Aunt Pearl had no peer among the good cooks in the Hicks' family. She prided herself on this. She wore out a cast iron wood stove large enough to land a 747. She replaced it at age 80 plus, stating to the family that if the second lasted as long as the first it would "get her to the grave." When the family bought her a new electric stove, she put it in the dining room and used it for a warming oven. It was only into her eighties that she gave up her cow and resorted to "store bought" dairy. While she had the cow on my visits I would "help" her churn butter.

Hicks Homeplace, circa 1800s

In her tiny kitchen was the mammoth wood stove with a hot water reservoir, a double dry sink with a farm pump, a large wooden bin with separators for her various flour, meal, etc. and an enamel top table for making biscuits. From this tiny enclave she could produce more food than most restaurants with a full staff. A standard Hicks' gathering at Aunt Pearl's included a midday (dinner) meal that consisted of boiled country ham, baked fresh ham, fried chicken, roast beef, cream potatoes, milk gravy, green beans, eastern North Carolina butterbeans, stewed tomatoes, sliced tomatoes, cucumbers, black-eyed peas, corn pudding, all accompanied by crackling cornbread and to die for sourdough hot biscuits. This feast was followed by Aunt Pearl's memorable homemade fresh coconut cake, chocolate cake and caramel cake. In the summer months hand turned ice cream nudged the cakes for recognition.

After the meal the men folk would smoke their "ready rolled" Camels and Luckys. Uncle Willy (Aunt Pearl's husband) always rolled his own. While the men smoked and drank steaming cups of dark rich coffee with chicory, the women folk cleared away the plates and silverware and assisted Aunt Pearl with cleaning up from the meal. The table was reset for the evening meal while Aunt Pearl, with experienced eyes, determined what food needed to be replenished and how many more biscuits were needed. The table was then covered with a large cheese cloth to await supper time.

In this recipe I chose Aunt Pearl's corn pudding to be the star. I created a corn pudding much akin to Aunt Pearl's dish but a half dozen clicks richer, creamier and more like a soufflé. You may wish to create this corn soufflé as part of a meal similar to the one described above and save enough for your dip. Making the banana pudding on page 112 as your dessert will give you the custard required for this recipe or you may simply use a like amount of Dannon La Crème brand vanilla yogurt with some Splenda to achieve a similar result. Two packs of Spenda to a four ounce package of yogurt should do it.

At a Hicks' gathering at Aunt Pearls, the taste of her corn pudding ranked with the great desserts on the sideboard. It is my fond wish that this corn soufflé will become one of your favorites. I think it's scrumptious and I hope you will too.

**3 cups fresh white corn (cut from cob) Note: 2 average ears of corn will
make a cup when cut from cob so figure 6 ears**
9 eggs (4 whole eggs and 5 additional egg yolks)
1½ cups white sugar
1½ tablespoons vanilla
3 tablespoons flour
¼ pound salted butter
2 cups half & half milk
1 teaspoon salt
½ teaspoon black pepper
5 ounces sharp white cheddar cheese
4 ounces cream cheese
**¼ cup boiled custard (see recipe on page 109) or a like amount of Dannon
La Crème brand vanilla yogurt**
**2 packs Splenda brand sweetener to a 4 ounce package of Dannon La
Crème brand vanilla yogurt (only if you are using yogurt instead of
boiled custard)**
¾ cup pecan pieces
1 teaspoon sea salt

Preheat oven to 350 degrees. Whisk eggs well. Melt butter in microwave for 1 minute and add the melted butter, half & half milk, corn, sugar, vanilla and dry ingredients to eggs. Whisk until blended well.

Place corn soufflé mixture into a greased (with butter) 9 inch by 12 inch baking dish. Fill a roasting pan half full with water and place soufflé baking dish in center of pan with water. Place into 350 degree oven and cook for approximately 60 minutes until soufflé is very lightly browned on top. Remove soufflé to rest and cool.

Toast nuts with sea salt over medium heat in medium-sized frying pan for about 3 minutes turning often until nuts are lightly browned. Remove nuts with slotted spoon.

Grate white cheddar cheese in food processor. Remove grated cheese from food processor and insert chopping blade. Replace grated cheese in food processor and add cream cheese in thumb-sized pinches. Add custard or yogurt. Important, if you are using yogurt in place of boiled custard then add Splenda to yogurt before adding to cheese mixture. Blend in food processor checking every 15 seconds until you achieve a smooth creamy dip consistency (about 30-45 seconds) that will hold on a cracker or rigid chip. Place cheese mixture into a large bowl. Add 3 cups of baked corn soufflé and fold. Add pecan pieces and fold. Total preparation time is approximately 1½ to 2 hours including cooking time for corn soufflé.

Makes 4 cups. Serve on water crackers.

SECTION 2

Shellfish and Fish Dips and Spreads

I have always had a fondness for crabs. When I was a small child my parents would visit Mr. and Mrs. Phales at their home on Masonboro Sound near Wrightsville Beach. The Phales' house sat on a hill overlooking the sound. At the foot of the hill was a small oyster house called Miss Janie's Oyster House. Miss Janie was in her eighties. She had two large mastiff dogs that could easily have inhaled me as an appetizer. Fortunately the dogs chose to be protective of me and Miss Janie.

I spent many hours sitting on the dock at Miss Janie's holding a piece of carpenter twine with a metal object tied to the end for a sinker and a loop knot about a foot above containing the bait and waiting for a blue crab to seize my offering. The string running over my index finger would alert me to the slightest tug. Once the crab seized the bait I would gently lift the string until the crab was just below the surface. A quick swoop of my wire net and I had another crab for my basket. Mrs. Phales would boil the crabs and we would sit around a large picnic table covered with newsprint, crack them with hammers and devour the delicious morsels with warm butter, crackers and sweet tea. Some of the crab meat was saved for Mrs. Phales to make her delicious she crab soup.

As a meal or served as an appetizer she crab soup is that wonder-

Mary Elizabeth, the author and Anna crabbing at Masonboro Sound, NC

ful, warm, rich, creamy concoction that evokes ummmmm's, ahhhhhh's and delights our palate. This recipe incorporates all the rich goodness of she crab soup and other supporting ingredients to make a dip that is so good, men pound the table and women swoon.

With more space and a few "cold ones" I would tell you the story about the time my friend and I were flounder gigging in the sound near Oregon Inlet and a giant crab caught our anchor rope and towed us out to open sea. By working feverishly with a fingernail clipper, we were finally able to cut our way through the anchor rope and return while we still had enough fuel to make shore.

First make Jim Early's She Crab Bisque. Enjoy the she crab bisque with lunch or dinner the day before you make the dip and save one cup for making the dip.

Jim Early's She Crab Bisque

1 can Harris brand she crab soup
1 can half & half milk (equal to amount of can of soup)
½ stick salted butter
3 teaspoons Frangelico liqueur
1 tablespoon parsley flakes
½ teaspoon cilantro flakes
½ teaspoon chives
½ teaspoon dill weed
3 dashes celery salt
3 dashes poppy seed
1 dash Mrs. Dash
1 dash Herbs de Province
2 tablespoons Jacques Cardin Napoleon Brandy

Into a 2 quart saucepan place contents of can of she crab soup. Add can of half & half milk. Stir over medium heat until all of the she crab soup is dissolved with the milk. Add butter in chips, Frangelico liqueur and herbs. Stir until all ingredients are well blended. Do not boil. Add brandy. Continue to stir until brandy is blended into the bisque.

Continue making Dip:

5 ounces sharp white cheddar cheese
4 ounces cream cheese
4 tablespoons sour cream
½ cup Jim Early's She Crab Bisque
1 package claw crabmeat (⅓ pound)
1 package jumbo lump crabmeat (⅓ pound)
3 tablespoons Grand Marnier liqueur
¼ stick unsalted butter
½ baseball-sized onion chopped medium (Rice Crispy-sized)
2 tablespoons chopped red bell peppers (about ¼ of pepper)
2 center cut slices of country ham

Grate cheddar cheese in large food processor. Remove grated cheese from food processor and insert chopping blade. Replace grated cheese in food processor and add cream cheese in pinches. Add sour cream and blend in food processor for about 30 seconds. Add Jim Early's She Crab Bisque and blend for about 15 seconds or until you achieve a smooth creamy dip consistency that will hold on a cracker or rigid chip. Remove cheese mixture to medium-large mixing bowl. Chop lump crab meat and add to mixture. Add claw crab meat and gently fold with rubber spatula. Add liqueur and fold gently with rubber spatula.

Melt butter in medium-sized pan over medium heat. Sauté chopped onions. Do not brown. Place sautéed onions and peppers in small food processor and buzz a couple of bursts. Add to mixture. Cook country ham per *Tips for Cooking* section at the end of this book. Remove all skin and fat from ham. Chop ham into small Rice Crispy-sized pieces. Remove mixture to large mixing bowl. Add ½ cup chopped ham and fold with whisk. Total preparation time is approximately 1 hour.

Makes 4 cups. Serve on water crackers.

SHRIMP, ARTICHOKE AND PISTACHIO NUT DIP

S ome of my fond memories of the North Carolina coast are associated with eastern North Carolina shrimparoos. Having several friends who are captains of commercial shrimp boats, access to fresh shrimp, heads on, right off the boat is not a problem. Having procured by purchase or barter a sufficient amount of fresh shrimp (I figure one pound per person) one only needs a clear night, a beach, a black iron cauldron, some firewood, a sauce pan, lots of butter, ears of corn in the husk, loads of French bread and a number three washtub filled with ice and longnecks of choice. Surround your feast with a circle of good friends who like to have a good time, kick off your sandals, crank up some good beach music and let the good times roll.

If the weather is inclement bring your party indoors, boil your shrimp in a big stock pot and pour onto a wooden table covered by newspaper. Add a few simple condiments such as melted butter and cocktail sauce, grab a paper plate and longneck and pig out. To round out this party one only needs a gathering of good

Shrimp boats, Oriental, NC

friends, a stack of beach music CDs (must include The Clovers Live at Myrtle Beach) and understanding neighbors. It's simple. It's easy. It's fun. It's wonderful! This recipe captures all the flavors of a true eastern North Carolina shrimparoo on a cracker.

½ pound medium-sized cooked, deveined, peeled and tailed shrimp
5 ounces sharp white cheddar cheese
4 ounces cream cheese
6 + heaping tablespoons sour cream
½ cup pistachio nuts
⅓ stick salted butter
1 teaspoon parsley flakes
½ teaspoon cilantro
2 pinches celery salt
½ teaspoon dill weed
½ teaspoon chives
¼ tablespoon poppy seed
½ tablespoon dill seed
½ teaspoon coarse cracked black pepper
1.4 ounces or ½ of 2.8 ounce pack Oscar Meyer Real Bacon Recipe brand
    bacon pieces
½ cup pistachio nuts
½ cup (about 3 +) jarred artichoke hearts (marinated in sunflower oil)

In large food processor grate cheddar cheese. Remove grated cheese from food processor and insert chopping blade. Replace grated cheese in food processor and add cream cheese in pinches. Add 6 heaping tablespoons sour cream and blend in food processor checking every 15 seconds until you achieve a smooth creamy dip consistency (approximately 30-45 seconds) that will hold on a cracker or rigid chip. If the blend is stiff add 2 more tablespoons sour cream one at a time. Remove cheese mixture to large mixing bowl. Set aside.

In a large fry pan melt butter in chips over medium heat. Place shrimp in pan (do not let shrimp overlap). Sprinkle shrimp with ½ teaspoon parsley flakes, ¼ teaspoon cilantro, ¼ teaspoon dill weed, 1 pinch celery salt and chives. Sauté shrimp, turning until well coated. Do not sauté shrimp more than 1-2 minutes as the shrimp are already cooked. Place 6-8 shrimp on cutting board and chop with chef's knife to medium chop (pea-sized). Repeat until all shrimp are chopped. Set aside.

In a small to medium-sized fry pan, warm the bacon pieces turning and separating for approximately 2-3 minutes. Place in bowl and set aside. Chop artichoke hearts on chopping board with chef's knife into M&M-sized pieces.

In a food chopper or small food processor chop ¼ cup pistachio nuts to medium chop (about ⅓ the original nut size). Repeat with the remaining pistachio nuts. Place chopped nuts in bowl and set aside.

Add shrimp to the cheese mixture and fold in with rubber spatula. Add chopped nuts and fold into mixture. Add poppy seed, dill seed, black pepper, ½ teaspoon parsley flakes, ¼ teaspoon cilantro, 1 pinch celery salt, ¼ teaspoon dill weed, bacon and artichoke pieces and fold until all ingredients are well blended. Total preparation time is approximately 30 minutes.

Makes 3 + cups. Serve on water crackers or Savory Thins brand crackers.

I would not suggest trying to make this spread hot as the shrimp does not have a strong enough flavor to stand up to really hot spices and will fade into the background leaving you with only a hot, spicy, nondescript dip which you can buy at any food store and save yourself some time.

Orleans

OYSTERS

Orleans

FANCY SMOKED

OYSTERS

SMOKED OYSTERS, PORTABELLA MUSHROOM AND WALNUT SPREAD

*O*ysters are one of my favorite shell fish. I like them raw on the half shell, lightly steamed, served oysters rockefeller, in stews and bisques. In fact if they are fresh and well prepared I feel about oysters like Mae West felt about men – I never met one I didn't like. I have enjoyed scrumptious oysters on the half shell while fishing and boating in the Chesapeake Bay area. I have enjoyed great oysters after a cold day in the duck blinds on the outer banks of North Carolina. I have enjoyed succulent oysters at some of the finest restaurants in Charleston, South Carolina and New Orleans, Louisiana.

Oriental Yacht Club
Oriental, NC

Whether savored in the ambiance of a regal four or five star restaurant, accompanied by a chilled bottle of Dom Pérignon or eaten in a more primitive fashion at a shuck your own oyster house outside a tiny hamlet along the coast, oysters are like chameleons – fitting nicely into whatever surroundings they are found. Some of my favorite oyster moments have been while quail hunting in the coastal areas near Oriental, North Carolina. During the lunch break I have gathered oysters with tongs from a jon boat, opened the shell, splashed Tabasco sauce, sprinkled salt and eaten them with a skinning knife and saltines. It doesn't get much better than that.

In this recipe I have used smoked oysters to eliminate some of the problems encountered with finding, preparing and preserving fresh oysters in an oyster spread.

One 3.75 ounce tin Smoked Oysters
One large 8 inch portabella mushroom cap
⅓ stick salted butter
1 teaspoon Jacques Cardin Napoleon Brandy
5 ounces sharp white cheddar cheese
4 ounces cream cheese
6 + heaping tablespoons sour cream
3 tablespoons English walnuts
1 teaspoon sea salt
4 tablespoons Oscar Meyer Real Bacon Recipe brand bacon pieces
1 teaspoon parsley flakes
1 teaspoon cilantro
1 teaspoon chives
¼ teaspoon dill weed
1 pinch celery salt

Remove oysters from packing oil. Chop oysters medium-fine in small food processor (buzz on low 2 or 3 short bursts). Set aside in small bowl.

Slice mushrooms into approximately ⅓ inch slices and trim. Melt butter in medium fry pan over medium heat. Place mushrooms in pan, add brandy, sauté and turn. Repeat. Total cooking time will take about 3 minutes. Remove and slice on cutting board with chef knife into Rice Crispy-sized pieces (make ½ cup chopped mushrooms).

In large food processor grate cheddar cheese. Remove grated cheese from food processor and insert chopping blade. Replace grated cheese in food processor and add cream cheese in pinches. Add 6 heaping tablespoons sour cream and blend in food processor checking every 15 seconds until you achieve a smooth creamy spread consistency (about 30-45 seconds) that will hold on a cracker or rigid chip. If the blend is stiff add 2 more heaping tablespoons of sour cream. Remove cheese mixture to large mixing bowl.

Fold in oysters with rubber spatula. Add mushrooms and fold. Add celery salt, parsley flakes, cilantro, chives, dill weed and fold.

Warm bacon pieces in medium fry pan over medium heat. Do not cook. Separate pieces with a fork. Stir and heat. Add bacon to mixture and fold. Toast nuts with sea salt over medium heat in medium-sized frying pan for about 3 minutes turning often until nuts are lightly browned. Add nuts and a little of the salt from the pan to mixture. Do not add much salt, certainly not all of it.

Fold bacon and nuts with mixture. The mixture should have a nice spread texture. If the mixture is still too stiff, add a little bit of sour cream 1 tablespoon at a time and work to desired texture. Total preparation time is approximately 30 minutes.

Makes 2 cups. Serve on water crackers.

Note: If you want this spread spicy, add crushed red pepper ½ tablespoon at a time until spread reaches the heat you desire. Don't add too much too quickly and rinse your palate between tastes or the pepper will come on quicker that you might expect. Also you do not want to overwhelm the oyster taste and end up with just another hot dip.

SCALLOP, GARLIC DILL AND MACADAMIA NUT DIP

*O*nce while fishing for halibut out of Homer Alaska, a trophy sized scallop took the bait. I thought I had snagged an anvil. The great scallop steadily pulled backwards as the boat traveled in the opposite direction, stripping line from my reel as the drag continued to whine. There were no aerobatic sail fish runs, no ICBM tarpon launches, just the unrelenting steady pull that kept the rod arched like a horseshoe. If you are still with me at this point I have some land in Florida I would like to discuss.

Sea scallops are one of those special offerings from our oceans. Possessed of firm white meat, the sea scallop has one of the more delicate tastes among shellfish and begs to be paired with a good white wine. Enjoy.

Salty Dawg Saloon, Homer Alaska

½ pound sea scallops
¼ pound salted butter
2 tablespoons salted butter (for sautéing onions)
1 teaspoon garlic salt
2 tablespoons chopped dill
1 teaspoon sea salt
5 ounces sharp white cheddar cheese
4 ounces cream cheese
4 tablespoons sour cream
½ baseball-sized onion medium chopped
1 center cut slice country ham
½ cup macadamia nuts

In a medium sauce pan melt ¼ pound butter over medium heat. Do not brown. Add scallops. Add garlic salt and dill. Cook for 10 minutes thoroughly coating scallops as you cook. Remove scallops from pan and save juices. With a chef's knife chop scallops medium-fine (M&M-sized pieces). Place in bowl, cover and set aside.

Grate cheddar cheese in food processor and remove to bowl. Change to chopping blade. Replace grated cheese in processor and add cream cheese in pinches. Add sour cream and blend in food processor checking every 15 seconds until you achieve a smooth creamy dip consistency (about 30-45 seconds) that will hold on a cracker or rigid chip. Remove cheese mixture from food processor to large mixing bowl. Add scallops to mixture. Fold in with rubber spatula. Add 2 tablespoons of cooking juice from scallops to mixture. Sauté onions and remaining 2 tablespoons of butter in small fry pan until onions are coated and tender. Add 2 tablespoons sautéed onions to mixture.

Cook country ham per *Tips for Cooking* section at the end of this book. Remove ham to cutting board. Trim away all fat and skin. Chop into medium-sized pieces (Rice Crispy/M&M). Add ½ cup chopped country ham to mixture. Toast nuts with sea salt over medium heat in medium-sized frying pan for about 3 minutes turning often until nuts are lightly browned. Remove nuts with slotted spoon and place in clean food processor. Chop nuts to approximately ¼ original size. Add nuts to mixture. Fold mixture with rubber spatula. Total preparation time is approximately 30 minutes.

Makes 3 cups. Serve on water crackers.

BABY CLAMS, PEPPERJACK CHEESE AND MACADAMIA NUT SPREAD

What can one say about baby clams? They are small, they are neither ugly nor attractive. There is little or no record of one having achieved great heights in learned professions, the performing arts or politics. They pretty much keep to themselves and only one or two have been connected with scandals that have made 60 Minutes. However, they are quite tasty when they are steamed and dipped in drawn butter. A full moon, good friends and a bon fire on the beach, accompanied by steamed clams and longnecks as a prelude to a lobster feast makes for a wonderful evening. This recipe captures those moments.

Prelude to a feast, Ocracoke, NC

4.5 ounce pepperjack cheese log
4 ounces cream cheese
5 heaping tablespoons sour cream
2 tablespoons medium-fine chopped green bell peppers (about ¼ of pepper)
2 tablespoons medium-fine chopped red bell peppers (about ¼ of pepper)
17 ounces drained chopped baby clams (Three and a half 5 ounce cans)
¼ stick salted butter
½ medium-sized onion chopped medium-fine (Rice Crispy-sized pieces)
2 ounces chopped macadamia nuts
½ tablespoon cilantro
1 tablespoon Herbs de Province
1 teaspoon dill seeds
4 teaspoons Texas Pete brand hot sauce

Grate pepperjack cheese in a large food processor. Remove grated cheese from food processor and insert chopping blade. Replace grated cheese in food processor and add cream cheese in pinches. Add sour cream and blend in food processor checking every 15 seconds until you achieve a smooth creamy spread consistency (about 30-45 seconds) that will hold on a cracker or rigid chip. Remove mixture to medium-large mixing bowl. Add green and red peppers and fold with rubber spatula. Add clams and fold with rubber spatula.

Chip butter and place in medium-sized frying pan. Add chopped onion and lightly sauté. Add 5 tablespoons sautéed onion to mixture and fold with rubber spatula. Add cilantro and fold with rubber spatula. Add Herbs de Province and fold with rubber spatula. Add dill seeds and fold with rubber spatula. Add Texas Pete and fold with rubber spatula. Add macadamia nuts and fold with rubber spatula.

Pepperjack is a rubbery cheese and does not lend itself to spreading well after being refrigerated. I suggest that you serve the spread at room temperature within a reasonable time after preparing. If you must refrigerate the spread before serving, microwave the spread in a bowl for about 20 seconds, separating and turning the spread with a rubber spatula at 7 second intervals. Total preparation time is approximately 30 minutes.

Makes 4 cups. Serve on water crackers.

SMOKED SALMON, CRACKED BLACK PEPPER, PINE NUTS AND CHAMPAGNE SPREAD

*I*f you have ever taken a salmon on the fly and felt the strength and shoulder of this great fish, you are indeed a lucky man or woman. Fly fishing for salmon in Alaska is one click short of heaven on earth for me. I have taken kings, cohoes, silvers and pinks on the fly with equal relish. I enjoy fishing for these great fish in remote lakes accessible only by float plane, from a riverboat or a two or three day raft float down a river. Or you can charter a helicopter with pontoons and get down on the deck and see a pod moving up the river, hopscotch ahead and catch and release them as they come through, mount up, hopscotch and do it all over again. After several hopscotches you will find that you have to hold your wrist with your free hand to control your rod. At this point its time to build that alder wood fire on the bank, pitch your tent, butterfly a couple of salmon on your grill, make some sourdough bread, pop the cap on a tall cool one and reflect on the beauty of your surroundings and how lucky a person you are to be alive and enjoying this special day.

This experience is equally rewarding on river banks in upstate New York or the banks of the River Tweed outside of Kelso, Scotland. Enjoying this feast with a friend, clinking longnecks and telling stories create the moments that keep you coming back again and again. When you serve this recipe, if you caught the salmon you will have stories to tell. If you bought the salmon, lying is optional. Enjoy!

5 ounces sharp white cheddar cheese
4 ounces cream cheese
4 heaping tablespoons sour cream
2 tablespoons chopped green bell peppers (about ¼ of pepper)
2 tablespoons chopped red bell peppers (about ¼ of pepper)
Two 4 ounce packages Echo Falls brand cracked pepper smoked salmon
½ cup pine nuts
1 teaspoon sea salt
½ medium-sized onion chopped
¼ stick salted butter
½ cup extra dry champagne

Grate cheddar cheese in large food processor. Remove grated cheese from food processor and insert chopping blade. Replace grated cheese in food processor and add cream cheese in pinches. Add sour cream and blend in food processor checking every 15 seconds until you achieve a smooth creamy spread consistency (about 30-45 seconds) that will hold on a cracker or rigid chip. Remove cheese mixture to medium-large mixing bowl. Add chopped red and green bell peppers and fold with rubber spatula. Remove smoked salmon to cutting board. Remove skin from salmon and discard. With chef's knife chop salmon into medium-sized pieces (size of a nickel) and add salmon to mixture. Fold gently with rubber spatula.

Toast nuts with sea salt over medium heat in medium-sized frying pan for about 3 minutes turning often until nuts are lightly browned. Remove nuts with slotted spoon. Chip butter, add to medium-sized fry pan and add chopped onion. Lightly sauté but do not overcook. Add onion to mixture and gently fold with rubber spatula. Add champagne and gently fold with rubber spatula. Add nuts and gently fold with rubber spatula. Total preparation time is approximately 30-35 minutes.

Makes 3 cups. Serve on water crackers.

SECTION 3

Cheese Dips and Spreads

BLUE CHEESE, GRAPES AND TOASTED
ENGLISH WALNUT/ALMOND DIP

ew cheeses impart that wonderful, robust, salty, pungent taste
and aroma that we associate with blue cheese. One of my favorite sandwiches is a ground sirloin burger infused with blue cheese, cooked medium-rare with strips of apple wood cured bacon, fresh crisp lettuce and a big slice of country tomato on a warm sesame seed bun with light mayo. Food for the gods.

A friend of mine once asked me to cook dinner for her mother who was coming to visit. I agreed and stated that I would fix a particular meal from one of my cooking classes. She responded, "Mother does not eat that." I offered yet another specialty and the response was, "Mother is allergic to that." After offering four or five different dinners that I cook particularly well with similar responses, I finally said, "Tell me what your mother likes and I will create a meal just for her." She said, "Mother likes tuna, bananas, grapes and nuts." With this as my marching orders I prepared a rather nice offering of pan seared sushi grade yellow fin tuna filets, seated on banana fosters syrup with red and white grapes and topped with warm blue cheese and sea salt toasted English walnuts. The saltiness of the walnuts and the blue cheese pair nicely with the banana fosters treatment of the grapes as a supporting cast for the beef like texture of the rare seared tuna. This offering was accompanied with a bundle of seven seasoned pan sautéed asparagus with a pimento wrap, a side of tiny red potatoes in a dill sauce and for the finale the baked apples with Jack Daniels and brown sugar dessert that appears in this book. The meal turned out rather nicely and "Mother" approved. Necessity is not only the mother of invention but sometimes the flame that sparks new recipes.

In this recipe I have cast the blue cheese in the starring role with a supporting cast that compliments the cheese in every scene.

8 ounces packaged blue cheese
8 ounces sharp white cheddar cheese
4 ounces cream cheese
3 heaping tablespoons sour cream
1 cup seedless red or white grapes
1 cup English walnuts or almonds
1 teaspoon sea salt

Crumble blue cheese and set aside. Grate white cheddar cheese in food processor. Remove grated cheese from food processor and insert chopping blade. Replace cheeses in food processor and then pinch cream cheese into teaspoon-sized pieces and add to white cheddar and blue cheese. Add sour cream and blend in food processor checking every 15 seconds until you achieve a smooth creamy dip consistency (about 30-45 seconds) that will hold on a cracker or rigid chip. Remove cheese mixture to large mixing bowl.

In clean food processor medium chop grapes into pieces ¼ to ⅛ of original size. Toast nuts with sea salt over medium heat in medium-sized frying pan for about 3 minutes turning often until nuts are lightly browned. Remove nuts with slotted spoon. Chop nuts in clean food processor to coarse chopped sized pieces. Gently fold chopped grapes and chopped nuts into cheese mixture. Do not blend with food processor, use a rubber spatula or whisk. Place in 4 or 8 ounce containers and cool in refrigerator. Total preparation time is approximately 20 minutes.

If you decide to use red grapes for this recipe I suggest you pair with English walnuts and if you decide to use white grapes I suggest pairing with almonds.

Makes 4 cups. Serve with non flavored chips with good rigidity or your favorite non flavored cracker.

JALAPEÑO PIMENTO CHEESE DIP
MILD I, SPICY II, HOT III

As a small child in an eastern North Carolina town, blustery winter Saturdays were spent "in camp." Camp was a "special place" behind the boarded walls of the attic, accessible by slithering through a small opening at the rafters onto an island of carefully spread planks over the ceiling joist. The "campfire" was provided by a vivid imagination and a five cell flashlight. A daisy chain of extension cords and an old Motorola radio provided all the entertainment a red-headed, freckled-faced, Opie looking 5 year-old cowboy could wish.

Saturday morning was the Buster Brown Show, sponsored by shoes of the same name. Each week Smiling Ed McCoy told stories to his sidekicks Froggy the Gremlin (Hi-ya kids! Hi-ya, Hi-ya, Hi-ya!) and Midnight the Cat (niceeee). My all time favorite story was Bomba the Jungleboy and his great Bull Elephant Tela. I can still hear the sound of Tela's trumpet. This Saturday ritual was regularly accompanied by three of my favorite "campfire" treats: My mother's homemade pimento cheese, homemade fried apple pies and cold fresh milk (our in-town neighbor had a cow and shared).

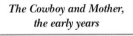

The Cowboy and Mother, the early years

Mother's pimento cheese was hand ground in a #2 Universal Sausage Grinder and made from a wheel of sharp cheddar cheese, pimento, Duke's Mayonnaise and black pepper. The apples for the pies came from the tree in our backyard and in season it was my duty to gather apples every morning and afternoon. The apples were peeled and sliced by Mother who arranged them on white sheets spread over adirondack chairs in the backyard to dry. The dried apples were then hung in cloth sacks for the winter. Mother's chunky pimento cheese spread thickly on Merita White Bread, warm golden brown fried apple pies and a big glass of cold milk from Henry Moss' cow (lowered over the attic wall by a loving mother who respected a cowboy's need for space) could turn a nasty winter day into a not-to-be forgotten memory.

Fifty plus years later on a Saturday when the wind is howling and sleet mixed with snow pelts the window pane and I cannot bird hunt, I long for my "camp," a thick pimento cheese sandwich, a fried apple pie, cold sweet milk and Tela.

Below is my mother's pimento cheese recipe with a half dozen modifications to transform it into an Old South comfort food with a New South twist.

---

1 pound extra sharp cheddar cheese
½ pound mild cheddar cheese
8 ounces cream cheese
8 rounded tablespoons mayonnaise
2 tablespoons worcestershire sauce
14 ounces jarred pimento pieces (drained)
14 ounces jarred roasted red peppers (drained)
3-6 ounces jarred jalapeño slices (drained)
1 cup cashew nuts
Two 2.8 ounce packages Oscar Meyer Real Bacon Recipe brand bacon
    pieces

Grind through sausage grinder, hand grate or process with food processor in grate mode the extra sharp cheddar cheese and mild cheddar cheese separately. Place sharp cheddar cheese and mild cheddar cheese in separate bowls. Into a large food processor with chopping blade inserted, place half of the sharp cheddar cheese, half of the mild cheddar cheese, half of the mayonnaise, half of the pimento pieces and half of the roasted red pepper pieces. Blend. Add half of the worcestershire sauce and half of the cream cheese in small pieces so as not to jam the food processor. Blend checking every 10 seconds until you have a smooth creamy dip consistency (approximately 20-30 seconds). You desire a dip consistency that will hold on a cracker or rigid chip.

Next add 1 ounce jalapeño slices for a mild dip, 2 ounces for a heartier dip and 3 ounces for a spicy dip. Blend. This blending should take approximately 10 seconds. Remove mixture to large mixing bowl. Repeat the blending process with the remaining half of your ingredients. My food processor will only hold half of this recipe at a time.

Remove half of your mixture to a large mixing bowl. Coarse chop the nuts and add half of the nuts to the mixture in your bowl. Warm half of the bacon pieces in a frying pan and add to mixture. Fold nuts and bacon into mixture with a rubber spatula. Repeat the nuts and bacon process with the remaining nuts and bacon pieces and add to the remaining half of your mixture and fold.

Store in tightly sealed containers (preferably glass) in refrigerator. Note: the taste of the jalapeños will intensify with overnight storage. To my taste the dip has a nice pimento cheese start and a jalapeño finish but not too lingering. I prefer the mild dip for a gathering with sweet iced tea, the heartier dip for a gathering with wine and the spicy dip for a gathering with longnecks. Total preparation time is approximately 25 minutes. Enjoy!

Makes 8 cups. Serve on water crackers, breadsticks or a non flavored chip with good rigidity.

MONTEREY JACK, BACON AND
PISTACHIO NUT DIP

The first time I married, my father was my best man. The second time I married this distinction befell my then college age son. As I recall, my energies the hour or so before the ceremony were spent trying to pry my best man away from watching a western movie on television for the third or fourth time and towards dressing for the event. It was the groom assisting the best man instead of vice versa. Having completed this task and dressing myself I turned to the dresser for my father's wedding band. I am allergic to jewelry and suggested to my bride-to-be that instead of her buying me a wedding band solely for the double ring ceremony, that we simply use my dad's ring for that purpose. It was gone. How, when, where – I will never know. I frantically searched under and around the dresser in vain but it was not to be found. Out of time! Must leave now! In a last minute makeshift move I took the keys from a split ring key holder and gave it to my son to give to the maid of honor, to give to the bride, to give to me.

When the minister at the appropriate time was handed the split key ring and unknowingly held it up and intoned, "This unbroken ring symbolizes the unbroken circle of love…" I thought my son would lose it.

Fortunately a wedding is the bride's day and no one was paying particular attention to the expression on my face and that of my son. A wink from me assured my lovely but puzzled bride that "all was well" and the wedding went off without a hitch.

My goal in this recipe was to showcase the cheese (the bride) without distractions from some of the ingredients (the groom and best man) and produce a good wedding party. I hope you agree. Enjoy.

½ pound grated Monterey Jack cheese (keep separate)

½ pound grated Monterey Jack cheese with jalapeño peppers (keep separate)

5 ounces grated sharp white cheddar cheese (keep separate)

10 heaping tablespoons of sour cream

1 tablespoon worcestershire sauce

1 tablespoon green olive juice

1 cup green olives with pimento centers chopped medium

1 cup shallot tops chopped with knife medium i.e. $\frac{1}{16}$

1 tablespoon jarred jalapeño peppers chopped fine (drained)

1.4 ounces or ½ 2.8 ounce package Oscar Meyer Real Bacon Recipe brand bacon pieces

2 cups pistachio nuts chopped medium-fine

1¾ cup half & half milk

Blend first 6 ingredients in food processor using chopping blade, checking every 15 seconds until you achieve a smooth creamy dip consistency (about 30-45 seconds) that will hold on a cracker or rigid chip. Remove mixture to large mixing bowl. Add olives and blend with rubber spatula. Add shallot tops and blend with rubber spatula.

Warm bacon pieces in medium fry pan over medium heat. Do not cook. Separate pieces with a fork. Stir and heat. Add bacon pieces to mixture. Blend remaining ingredients with rubber spatula. Use 1¾ cups of half & half milk to thin. Blend with rubber spatula until folded in nicely or thin with white wine. Total preparation time is approximately 25 minutes.

Makes 4 cups. Serve on water crackers, plain bagel crisps, plain pita chips or breadsticks.

THREE CHEESES, GREEN ONION AND
GARLIC ROASTED PINE NUT DIP

I like to hunt Appalachian Ruffed Grouse. Some of my favorite areas are upper peninsula Michigan, Maine and certain areas of the mountains of North Carolina. One of the areas of our mountains that is a favorite of mine is a little community called Lansing in Ashe County. This area holds a number of good grouse lots and is the home of the only cheese making company in the Old North State.

Ashe County Cheese is located in West Jefferson, a small mountain town at the foot of Mt. Jefferson. I have had the pleasure of visiting this store many times while grouse hunting, fly fishing, messing about the area on picnics or dining at Shataly Springs or my favorite mountain hideaway – The Riverhouse. I guess it is the little boy in me that likes to see the cheese being made. It is a treat to watch this process and then step across the street to the main store and purchase the finished product along with any number of other delectable items from our mountains. I think we are fortunate to have a cheese making company in our area and it affords school children and adults an opportunity to see a food making process that generally occurs in states far to our north. Ashe County Cheese makes good cheese in a number of varieties. It seems even more special when you have watched it come to life. Try some!

I never visit Ashe County Cheese without being reminded of that old Southern fairy tale about The Three Little Cheeses. It goes like this…

Once upon a time there were three little cheeses – brothers. The youngest cheese, Lil' Yellow, was a mild cheddar who was a bit of a bookworm and given to fantasy. The middle cheese, Whitey, was a sharp cheddar with a reputation for slick dealing and the truth was not in him. The senior sibling, Ole' Blue, was wise beyond his years, possessed of strong opinions and lived large.

The three cheeses decided to build homes in Cheeseboro, a bedroom community to a large Southern city. Lil' Yellow built a thatched affair of cheese straws. Whitey built on the lake. His was a rustic dwelling constructed of cheese logs chinked with Cheese Wiz. Ole' Blue built a colonial monstrosity of cheese bricks with cream cheese columns. Ole' Blue also installed a security system that made Fort Knox look like a tree house.

All went well with the brothers until Clyde the cheese monster, the biggest, baddest cat you have ever seen, returned from pillaging other villages in the area. Now Clyde had a thing for cheese and he drooled as he laid his fiendish plans for the three little cheeses. Clyde came calling. Not one to huff and puff, Clyde cut to the chase and advised Lil' Yellow that if Lil' Yellow did not pay the cheese ransom Clyde demanded, that Clyde would "Bite his face off." This message was repeated at the homes of the other two little cheeses.

One of the three little cheeses became a spread, one became a fondue and guess which one lived happily ever after. Wrong! It seems that Lil' Yellow, the mild one, was also a sorcerer and made himself into a beautiful princess, married Clyde, drug him through divorce court and now lives in a villa in Switzerland with the handsome contractor that built Ole' Blue's house and slipped Clyde the security code for the princess' phone number.

Don't you just love fairy tales with happy endings?

This recipe simply combines three of my favorite cheeses (without all the drama) with some of my favorite condiments such as onions, garlic and roasted pine nuts. This recipe makes a nice offering for all occasions running the gamete from longnecks to fine wine. It is simple. It is easy to make and generally enjoyed by all.

2 ounces packaged blue cheese
4 ounces sharp white cheddar cheese
4 ounces mild yellow cheddar cheese
5 heaping tablespoons sour cream
2 heaping tablespoons mayonnaise
2 tablespoons finely chopped spring onion bulbs
2 tablespoons medium chopped spring onion tops
1 teaspoon garlic salt
¼ cup pine nuts
12 green olives with pimento centers medium chopped
1 tablespoon worcestershire sauce

Crumble blue cheese and set aside. Grate white and yellow cheddar cheeses. Remove grated cheeses from food processor and insert chopping blade. Replace grated cheeses in food processor and add crumbled blue cheese, sour cream, mayonnaise and worcestershire sauce. Blend in food processor checking every 15 seconds until you achieve a smooth creamy dip consistency (about 30-45 seconds) that will hold on a cracker or rigid chip. Remove cheese mixture to large mixing bowl and add spring onion tops, bulbs, olives and fold.

Toast nuts with garlic salt over medium heat in medium-sized frying pan for about 3 minutes turning often until nuts are lightly browned. Remove nuts with slotted spoon. Fold nuts into cheese dip with rubber spatula. Total preparation time is approximately 20 minutes.

Makes 16 ounces. Serve on water crackers, plain bagel crisps, plain pita chips or breadsticks.

PARMESAN CHEESE, SUN DRIED TOMATOES, PEPPERONI AND PISTACHIO NUT DIP

*P*izza is one of the most popular casual foods in the country. Though not indigenous to the Old South, pizza certainly has a following in the New South. Few people under mandatory retirement age have not enjoyed this hot, aromatic, taste tripping offering we call pizza pie. Be it round or square, thick crust or thin crust, Italian, Sicilian or variations on a theme – across the country people seem to associate pizza with good friends and good times. The New South is no different. Number me as one of the soldiers in that army. I LIKE PIZZA! Generally I order the supreme with everything on it including the kitchen sink and anchovies. A good hot pizza pie, great friends and pitchers of cold beer make for a fun evening in any setting.

In this recipe I have tried to capture that wonderful flavor of a really well made cheese, tomato sauce and pepperoni pizza. I admit being a bit partial to the thin crust pizza as I believe it delivers the ingredients better without infusing too much bread taste. I hope this dip conjures up some good memories from high school, college, sports events or wherever you had pizza and good times.

8 ounces white cheddar cheese
8 ounces fresh parmesan cheese in block
4 ounces cream cheese
½ cup sun dried tomatoes
5 heaping tablespoons sour cream
1 cup medium chopped pistachio nuts
½ cup thin sliced pepperoni
4 ounces roasted red peppers
2 tablespoons jarred chopped jalapeño peppers (drained)
1 tablespoon medium chopped green olives
1 tablespoon black olive tapenade

Spread pepperoni slices on a 12 inch by 24 inch cookie sheet. Place in oven on broil for 2 minutes. Do not overcook. Pat dry pepperoni between paper towels. Cut pepperoni into slices $\frac{1}{8}$ their original size.

In food processor grate parmesan and white cheddar cheeses. Remove grated cheeses from food processor and insert chopping blade. Replace grated cheeses in food processor and add sour cream and cream cheese in teaspoon-sized pinches. Add roasted peppers to cheese mixture and blend in food processor checking every 15 seconds until you achieve a smooth creamy dip consistency (about 30-45 seconds) that will hold on a cracker or rigid chip. Add jalapeño peppers to mixture and blend just long enough to mix them into the mixture. Remove mixture to large mixing bowl. Fold in tomatoes, pepperoni, pistachio nuts, green olives and black olive tapenade. Total preparation time is approximately 30 minutes.

Makes 4+ cups. Serve on plain crackle crackers or New York style plain bagel chips.

PEPPERJACK, SHALLOT AND PINE NUT DIP

*E*ach time I taste or smell pepperjack cheese my senses whisk me away to a small hotel overlooking the sea in Monterey, California. It was late afternoon and I had opted to shoot film instead of eat lunch. I wanted something but did not want to spoil my dinner plans at the Sardine Factory that evening. To stave off my hunger pangs I chose a bit of cheese and wine. The wine was a rich full bodied red with good tannins and taste of currants. The cheese was pepperjack.

Sardine Factory, Monterey California. Reprint courtesy of Bert Cutino

I recall the immense feeling of warmth that I experienced from the earth tones of the adobe and tile terrace, the rays of the sun, the gentle breezes from the sea and the kaleidoscope of soft pale hues from the curling edge of twilight.

It was a very peaceful and quiet time, broken only by the cries of the gulls, the sigh of the sea and the splashing of the sea otters as they played among the shafts of light. Though many years have passed, on a day fraught with frustration and nerves occasionally frayed, I can close my eyes in the midst of the storm and go to this quiet retreat and mentally enjoy the sights, the sounds, the smells and the taste of good wine and cheese at this special place.

CAUTION: This is the <u>HOT</u> version. You may wish to start with 1/3 the suggested amount of crushed hot red pepper and 1/3 the suggested amount of jalapeños. You can always ratchet it up at the end for a hotter dip.

7 ounces pepperjack cheese
7 ounces sharp white cheddar cheese
6 heaping tablespoons sour cream
8 heaping tablespoons mayonnaise
$\frac{1}{4}$ cup chopped green bell pepper (M&M-sized pieces)
$\frac{1}{4}$ cup chopped red bell pepper (M&M-sized pieces)
1 tablespoon worcestershire sauce
2 tablespoons crushed hot red pepper
$\frac{1}{2}$ cup jarred jalapeño slices (drained)
One 2.8 ounce package Oscar Meyer Real Bacon Recipe brand bacon
   pieces
$\frac{3}{4}$ cup pine nuts (22-23 ounces)
$\frac{1}{2}$ teaspoon garlic salt
$\frac{1}{2}$ cup shallots

Grate pepperjack cheese in food processor, remove and set aside. Grate cheddar cheese in food processor, remove and set aside. Insert chopping blade into food processor. Replace grated cheeses in food processor and add sour cream and mayonnaise. Blend checking every 15 seconds until you achieve a smooth creamy dip consistency that will hold on a cracker or rigid chip (about 30-45 seconds).

Chop jalapeño slices in small food processor or by hand. Add to mixture. Add bell peppers, worcestershire sauce and red pepper to mixture. Blend just enough to mix peppers and spices into mixture. Remove cheese mixture to a large mixing bowl. Heat bacon pieces in medium frying pan over medium heat for 2-3 minutes. Add bacon pieces to mixture and fold with rubber spatula.

Toast nuts with garlic salt over medium heat in medium-sized frying pan for about 3 minutes turning often until nuts are lightly browned. Add nuts and salt to mixture and fold with rubber spatula. Chop shallots on cutting board with chef's knife. Add shallots to mixture and fold.

If you would like this dip hotter, add 1 tablespoon of hot sauce at a time to reach desired heat. Serve with tongs and lead apron and have guests sign release before party.

Pepperjack is a rubbery cheese and does not lend itself to spreading well after being refrigerated. I suggest that you serve the dip at room temperature within a reasonable time after preparing. If you must refrigerate the dip before serving, microwave the dip in a bowl for about 20 seconds, separating and turning the dip with a rubber spatula at 7 second intervals. The dip should be served soft on water crackers with a favorite wine. I prefer a red to a white with this one. Total preparation time is approximately 30 minutes.

Makes 4 cups. Serve on water crackers, plain bagel chips, breadsticks, plain pita chips or stuff into roasted mild chili peppers.

SECTION 4

Fruits and Berries Dips and Spreads

STRAWBERRY, WHITE CHEDDAR CHEESE AND CASHEW DIP

*F*or those who like the slightly sweet, slightly tangy taste of ripe strawberries – this is your dip. In my neck of the woods there are a number of strawberry farms that allow you to pick your own berries. I have fond memories of taking my youngest child Mary Elizabeth strawberry picking when she was quite small. She seemed particularly fascinated to find these treats growing within her grasp. Watching her face as she filled her basket and her pleasure when she found an unusually large berry is one of the fond memories from my treasure chest of her childhood.

Strawberries that have been allowed to field ripen are a much sweeter better fruit than strawberries picked prematurely for shipping to markets. Whether you pick your berries or buy them from the market, I think you're going to like this one. This dip, slightly warmed, is wonderful over cheesecake.

Mary Elizabeth in the Strawberry Patch

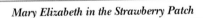

5 ounces sharp white cheddar cheese
4 ounces cream cheese
Two 6 ounce cups of strawberry yogurt (12 ounces)
3 tablespoons sweetened condensed milk
5 tablespoons strawberry preserves
1 cup fresh strawberries washed, capped, cored and chopped medium
1 cup salted cashew nuts
4 tablespoons Frangelico liqueur

Grate white cheddar cheese in large food processor. Remove grated cheese from food processor and insert chopping blade. Replace grated cheese in food processor and add cream cheese in pinches (half thumb size). Add yogurt and blend in food processor checking every 15 seconds until you achieve a smooth creamy dip consistency (about 30-45 seconds) that will hold on a thin cookie or wafer. Remove mixture to a medium-large mixing bowl. Add condensed milk and fold gently with rubber spatula. Add strawberry preserves and fold gently.

Cap (and if the berries are larger, quarter berries and cut away pulp) and chop berries gently by hand in medium bowl. You should have 1 cup of chopped berries when done. Gently fold the berries into the mixture.

Place ¼ cup cashews in small food processor and buzz on high speed. Check for consistency; you want to have medium pieces. Repeat 4 times. Add 1 cup chopped nuts to mixture. Fold gently so that you do not crush berries. Add liqueur and fold gently turning mixture as you fold, being careful not to crush berries. Total preparation time is approximately 30-35 minutes.

Makes 3½ cups. Serve on thin wafer or cookie of your choice.

BLACKBERRY, BOYSENBERRY, BRIE AND WALNUT DIP

My mother made a blackberry cobbler that was second to none. From time to time I had the opportunity to pick the berries. My first memory of picking blackberries came from an invitation by a neighbor to accompany him "up to the country" to pick berries. He was a nice man and a long-time neighbor. I was pleased to bring Mother a full pail of luscious vine-ripened berries. I was unaware, until hours later, that I also brought home "chiggers." After two or three days of lying on my bed slathered in calamine lotion, my agony passed as did my newly acquired enhancements and the thoughts that at ten years old I might be the next male adult movie star. Unless you are well protected with insect spray I suggest you acquire your blackberries from the market. No cobbler or dip is worth the experience I just described.

---

8 ounces brie cheese
4 ounces cream cheese
Two 6 ounce cups Dannon brand boysenberry yogurt (12 ounces)
½ cup English walnuts (chopped)
½ cup black walnuts (chopped)
1 teaspoon sea salt
4 tablespoons blackberry preserves
2 cups fresh blackberries
4 tablespoons sugar

Tear brie into medium-sized pieces (pecan size). Place brie into large food processor with chopping blade inserted. Add cream cheese in pinches. Add yogurt and blend in 15 second bursts, being careful not to puree the brie, until you achieve a smooth creamy dip consistency (about 30-45 seconds) that will hold on a thin cookie or wafer. Remove mixture to medium large mixing bowl. Add blackberry preserves to mixture and fold with rubber spatula.

Toast nuts with sea salt over medium heat in medium-sized frying pan for about 3 minutes turning often until nuts are lightly browned. Remove nuts with slotted spoon. Add nuts and fold in gently.

Place 1 cup of fresh blackberries into medium bowl and hand-cut berries into medium pieces (¼ size of whole berry). Repeat with second cup. Add 2 tablespoons of sugar to each cup of chopped berries and fold lightly with fork. Repeat with remaining 2 tablespoons of sugar and remaining cup of berries. Add berry mixture and fold very gently with rubber spatula. Total preparation time is approximately 30-35 minutes.

Makes 4 cups. Serve on thin shortbread type cookies of choice.

BLUEBERRY AND ROASTED CHESTNUT DIP

*B*lueberries are just plain scrumptious. I like picking wild berries while hiking and fishing in Maine. I like to see their dark eyes peering out from sourdough pancakes at Jedediah's House of Sourdough in Jackson Hole, Wyoming. I like them in pies, cheesecake and muffins. I like them on homemade vanilla custard ice cream.

Just outside of Hertford, North Carolina (Hertford is the home-town of Catfish Hunter of Yankees' pitching fame) is a bed and breakfast called Beechtree Inn. This charming stopover consists of the main house and a compound of restored 1700s circa cabins reconstructed by the owners Ben and Jackie Hobbs with carefully hidden modern amenities. Ben is a master furniture craftsman and has a woodworking school on site. All of the furniture in the cabins consist of correct period reproductions for each particular cabin. The ambience and quietness of this rural Southern place creates heaven on earth for a writer or anyone seeking a quiet place to create or play. When I was first there the lady of the manor was also the chief cook and bottle washer. Now the inn has a restaurant in a restored building and a new chef.

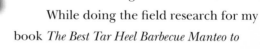

Sunset Cape Elizabeth, Maine

While doing the field research for my book *The Best Tar Heel Barbecue Manteo to Murphy* it was my good fortune to find this place and spend some time. To my delight my first breakfast consisted of made from-scratch pancakes with blueberries picked from the yard that morning. This wonderful offering was accompanied with homemade sausage (from a farmer down the road) and cups of steaming black coffee along with homemade jams, jellies, etc. What a lovely treat, this place – and what gracious hosts.

It was my intent that in this recipe the blueberries take center stage and dance with a small supporting cast that lets them shine. Enjoy!

---

10 ounces sharp white cheddar cheese
4 ounces cream cheese
One 8 ounce cup Breyer's Crème Savers Blueberries and Crème brand
     yogurt
2 teaspoons blueberry preserves
1 cup chestnuts
½ cup fresh blueberries
1 teaspoon sea salt
1 teaspoon sugar
2 sprays butter flavored cooking spray

Grate white cheddar cheese in food processor. Remove grated cheese from food processor and insert chopping blade. Replace grated cheese in food processor and add cream cheese in teaspoon-sized pieces. Add yogurt, preserves and blend in food processor checking every 15 seconds until you achieve a smooth creamy dip consistency (about 30-45 seconds) that will hold on a thin cookie or wafer.

Toast nuts with sea salt over medium heat in medium-sized frying pan for about 3 minutes turning often until nuts are lightly browned. Remove nuts with slotted spoon and dump salt in trash. Replace nuts in frying pan and spray lightly with butter spray. Coat nuts in pan with sugar. Warm nuts for 1 or 2 minutes but do not brown or cook nuts. Remove nuts with slotted spoon, place into clean food processor and buzz several times to obtain a coarse chop. Place fresh blueberries in clean food processor and buzz several times to coarse chop the berries into pieces approximately ⅓ or ½ their original size.

Into a large mixing bowl place the cheese and yogurt mixture. Gently fold the chestnut praline pieces and chopped blueberries into the mixture with a rubber spatula. Total preparation time is approximately 30-35 minutes.

Makes 28 ounces. Serve at room temperature with ginger almond cookies or your cookie of choice.

APRICOT, HONEY AND
TOASTED ALMOND DIP

I admit to not being a big apricot fan as a child. At that time in my life apricots were only a click above brussels sprouts on my list of least favorite foods. As I recall my first encounter with an apricot was in the form of stewed apricots, much akin to stewed apples. I thought I was being punished. I hid some of my serving under a biscuit half and washed the rest of my portion down with great gulps of milk. I think I expected to get an orange slice which usually followed a dose of castor oil. No such luck.

However, with some birthdays and developing a more adventurous palate, I have learned to like this fruit quite well. I now use this fruit in a number of dishes and find it delightful in the form of jams, jellies and preserves. Apricot preserves atop a hot sourdough biscuit half slathered with soft country butter makes a pretty neat finish to a country supper.

This recipe brings together cheeses that do not overwhelm the delicate taste of an apricot and a number of ingredients that I think enhance the taste of the apricot without stealing scenes.

---

5 ounces sharp white cheddar cheese
4 ounces cream cheese
4 tablespoons sour cream
1 cup dried apricot
4 tablespoons pure raw honey
½ cup toasted almond pieces
3 tablespoons Grand Marnier liqueur

Grate cheddar cheese in a large food processor. Remove grated cheese from food processor and insert chopping blade. Replace grated cheese in food processor and add cream cheese in pinches. Add sour cream and blend in food processor checking every 15 seconds until you achieve a smooth creamy dip consistency (about 30-45 seconds) that will hold on a thin cookie or wafer.

With a chef's knife slice dry apricots into small slices about the size of Rice Crispies. Slice 1 cup and set aside.

Remove cheese mixture to medium-large mixing bowl. Add apricots and fold with rubber spatula. Add honey and fold with rubber spatula. Add almonds and gently fold with rubber spatula. Add liqueur and fold in gently. Total preparation time is approximately 30 minutes.

Makes 2½ cups. Serve on thin butter cookies of choice.

CANTALOUPE, BACON AND PISTACHIO NUT DIP

About 8 miles east of my hometown of Henderson, North Carolina lies another small eastern North Carolina town called Ridgeway. Ridgeway is the self-proclaimed cantaloupe capital of the world. This may or may not be the case but I have never found reason to question this claim. I have been content simply to live close to the source of the best cantaloupe that I have ever tasted.

I have purchased a number of cantaloupes from high end food stores and "fresh markets" in various locations. The melons that I purchased, in my opinion, do not come close to the wonderful sweet taste of the melons I enjoyed as a child. My grandfather who lived next door was a stickler for fresh food and certain brand names. Papa Hicks, though he lived in town, had his own smokehouse in the backyard. In this house hung some of the best hams, shoulders and side meat produced in eastern North Carolina. Papa Hicks had a particular farmer who raised his pigs a certain way, cured his meat in a certain fashion and delivered the end product to my grandfather. He had certain people in the country that regularly brought fresh vegetables to the house. He would only buy Dukes mayonnaise, Lea & Perrins worcestershire sauce, White Lilly flour and Luzianne coffee with chicory – and of course his cantaloupes had to come from Ridgeway.

As a small child I remember riding each week to Ridgeway when cantaloupes were in season for Papa Hicks to select the melons for the week. These melons were vine-ripened and picked at first light on the morning they were sold. They were sold from roadside stands operated by the farmer or members of his family. Naturally Papa Hicks would only buy from one particular farmer whom he believed grew the sweetest and the best melons. At a very early age I was taught how to smell the melon where the stem was removed and to "feel of it" and give it the proper "thump" to assure it had reached the peak of perfection before it was added to our crate.

Before we moved to Winston-Salem, my dad had a fleet of trucks that hauled tobacco in hogsheads during tobacco season and cantaloupes from Ridgeway to New York City during melon season. Dad had many stories to tell about what was required to "do business" on the waterfront in New York City, especially if you were hauling cantaloupes with trucks bearing North Carolina license plates. There was a tariff.

Whether brought home by Dad or Papa Hicks, cantaloupes were a large part of our table fare during melon season. It's hard to beat a breakfast of country ham, fresh eggs, grits, cantaloupe, homemade country butter, hot sourdough biscuits, pear preserves, and strong coffee. Cantaloupe was also served with fresh vegetables, spoon bread and sweet tea for a meatless supper on a warm summer evening.

In this dip I have tried to recapture some of the memories described above and added some ingredients that I think go well with my favorite melon. This dip is best served the day made. Treat yourself.

---

5 ounces sharp white cheddar cheese
4 ounces cream cheese
2 cups chopped cantaloupe
½ cup chopped pistachio nuts (chopped medium)
1 cup Oscar Meyer Real Bacon Recipe brand bacon pieces
1 tablespoon sweet basil leaves finely chopped
½ tablespoon truffle oil
1 tablespoon almond syrup
½ cup almonds
6 or more packages Splenda brand sweetener (to taste)
1 teaspoon sea salt
8 + ounces Dannon La Crème brand vanilla yogurt
1 tablespoon Fruit Fresh produce protector

Place 1 cup chopped cantaloupe in a bowl, sprinkle with ½ tablespoon Fruit Fresh and toss together. In a food processor grate cheddar cheese. Remove grated cheese from food processor and insert chopping blade. Replace grated cheese in food processor and add cream cheese in thumb-sized pinches. Add 1 cup chopped cantaloupe to cheese mixture and blend in food processor checking every 15 seconds until you achieve a smooth creamy dip consistency (about 30-45 seconds) that will hold on a thin cookie or wafer. Remove cheese mixture to medium bowl. In a medium frying pan over medium heat, heat bacon pieces for 3 minutes turning often with a fork. Add pistachio nuts, bacon pieces, truffle oil and fold. Add basil and fold. Add almond syrup and fold.

Toast almonds with sea salt over medium heat in medium-sized frying pan for about 3 minutes turning often until nuts are lightly browned. Remove nuts with slotted spoon. Buzz almonds in a small food processor until the nuts are about ¼ of their original size, add to mixture and fold. With a chef's knife chop the remaining 1 cup of cantaloupe into raisin-sized pieces. Place chopped cantaloupe in a bowl, sprinkle with remaining ½ tablespoon Fruit Fresh and toss together. Add cantaloupe to mixture and gently fold. Add Splenda and fold. You may wish to add more Splenda depending on the ripeness and sweetness of your cantaloupe and your personal preference. Add 8 ounces yogurt and fold. If dip is too tight, add more yogurt 1 tablespoon at a time to reach desired consistency. Total preparation time is approximately 30 minutes.

Makes 3½ cups. Serve on water crackers.

SUN DRIED FIGS, BRIE AND PISTACHIO NUT DIP

As a young boy we had a fig tree of enormous proportions that grew up to a second story window of our home. I could climb out of my bedroom window onto the roof and shimmy down the fig tree to my steed (Columbia bicycle) and be gone before I could have made it down the stairs and out the door. Sometimes this was good, sometimes not. To protect the figs from the starlings and other feathered raiders, I devised a system with tin cans holding a few pieces of gravel that were tied to branches and a window weight cord tied to limbs running through my bedroom window. A few jerks on the cord would empty the tree of bandits. If this did not make a sufficient impression on the fig thieves, I resorted to plan B – my Daisy Red Ryder BB carbine.

My mother made the best fig preserves from our tree that I have ever tasted. The preserves were served with hot made-from-scratch biscuits for which Mother had no peer. This recipe brings back childhood memories of hot biscuits, fig preserves, Red Ryder and his sidekick Little Beaver.

8 ounces brie cheese
4 ounces cream cheese
4 heaping tablespoons sour cream
6-8 calimyrana figs
3 tablespoons fig preserves
3 tablespoons Frangelico liqueur
½ cup pistachio nuts

Break brie cheese into whole pecan-sized pieces. Place brie cheese in large food processor with chopping blade inserted. Add cream cheese in pinches, sour cream and blend.

In a small food processor place 3 to 4 figs. Chop figs and remove. Repeat. 6

to 8 figs should produce ½ cup of chopped figs. Add chopped figs to cheese mixture. Add fig preserves and blend. Do not over-blend. You should buzz, stop and taste; buzz, stop and taste. When you have a nice thick creamy spread with good brie presence and the accompanying sweet fig taste, you have arrived!

Remove mixture to large mixing bowl. Add liqueur and fold with rubber spatula. Place nuts in small food processor. You should buzz, stop, buzz, stop – so that you are just breaking up some of the nuts, but not all. Don't make meal. Add nuts to mixture and fold with rubber spatula. Total preparation time is approximately 30-35 minutes.

Makes 3 cups. Serve on thin non fruit flavored cookie of choice that most closely resembles a good biscuit. Or serve on something from the baker that does not have a competing flavor.

BARTLETT PEAR, STILTON CHEESE AND TOASTED HAZELNUT DIP

In our house the shining star of all of my mother's preserve making was her pear preserves. Mother never comprehended making anything in small amounts. She was always prepared for the 82nd Airborne to parachute into the backyard and to feed them well and send them off with to-go bags. Mother made pear preserves in a gargantuan pot on the stove. She stirred with a hand-carved wooden paddle made for stews. I can still smell the wonderful aroma of the pears in bubbling syrup from Mother's kitchen. When Mother had packaged her preserves in pint-sized Mason jars, she would always spoil me by honoring my request that she overcook some of the syrup until it was so thick it would stand a spoon. When cooled this pear flavored treat could be roped on a tablespoon and became the pear flavored forerunner of the Sugar Daddy. This recipe is a company of one of my favorite cheeses, one of my favorite fruits and a host of other goodies. They dance well together.

Mother, age 17

¹⁄₃ **pound stilton cheese**
4 ounces cream cheese
Two 4 ounce cups Dannon la Crème brand vanilla yogurt (8 ounces)
¹⁄₂ **pound or** ¹⁄₂ **jar Del Monte Orchard Select brand sliced Bartlett pears**
    (makes 1 cup medium chopped)
4 tablespoons sweet orange marmalade
4 ounces chopped hazelnuts
1 teaspoon sea salt

Break stilton cheese into marble-sized pieces and place into large food processor with chopping blade inserted. Add cream cheese in pinches. Add yogurt and blend in food processor checking every 15 seconds until you achieve a smooth creamy dip consistency (about 30-45 seconds) that will hold on a thin cookie or wafer. Remove mixture to medium-large mixing bowl.

With fork remove 8 ounces of pears from jar. You do not want to bring syrup so don't use spoon to remove pears. Place pears in medium-sized mixing bowl. Hold a slice of pear with a fork and slice long ways with paring knife Chop pears into thumb-nail-sized pieces. Do not smush the pears. Add pear pieces to mixture and fold gently with rubber spatula. Add marmalade and fold gently.

Toast nuts with sea salt over medium heat in medium-sized frying pan for about 3 minutes turning often until nuts are lightly browned. Remove nuts with slotted spoon. Add nuts to mixture and fold gently. Total preparation time is approximately 40-45 minutes.

Makes 3 cups. Serve on water crackers, plain toasted rounds or shortbread cookie of choice.

WILD BING CHERRIES, GOAT CHEESE AND TOASTED ENGLISH WALNUT DIP

I am crazy about the South, but I must confess that Montana trips my trigger. Whether I am snowmobiling in Lincoln, fly fishing one of its famous rivers, chasing critters with a camera in the high country or kicked back around a campfire with old friends – I know that this has got to be one of the "last best places."

In addition to its great fisheries and host of wildlife, Montana also produces some delectable fruits and berries. Bing cherries grow in abundance outside of Polson, Montana. The brave souls that pick them should probably receive hazardous duty pay for having to compete with the bears for this delicacy. A great day for me is to visit my artist buddies in the area and see what they have painted or sculpted since my last visit. No visit to this area would be complete for me without spending some time on Flathead Lake with a really fast boat and a picnic consisting of elk tenderloin medallions, sourdough rolls, a good red wine, freshly picked wild bing cherries and custard ice cream.

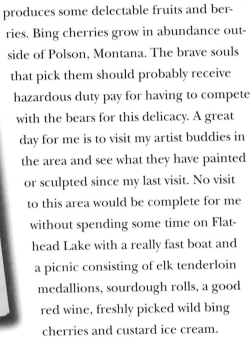

Author in Lincoln, Montana

Should you desire to have this experience, boats are available at the marina at the bridge in Polson and Wild Horse Island is a good destination on the lake. Sharing a picnic in this place with someone special under a Montana sky makes heaven seem not so far away.

8 ounces goat cheese
8 ounces cream cheese
12 ounces Dannon la Crème brand vanilla yogurt
3 ounces sun dried bing cherries
½ cup English walnuts
One 8 ounce cup Breyers Crème Savers brand raspberries and crème yogurt
1 teaspoon sea salt
2 tablespoons Grand Marnier liqueur
8 packages Splenda brand sweetner

Break goat cheese into thumb-sized pieces and place in large food processor with chopping blade inserted. Add cream cheese in pinches. Add vanilla yogurt and blend in food processor checking every 15 seconds until you achieve a smooth creamy dip consistency (about 30-45 seconds) that will hold on a thin cookie or wafer.

Place 1 ounce of cherries in small food processor and chop on high speed until cherries are ½ to ⅓ of original size. Repeat with remaining cherries. Add all cherries to cheese mixture. Buzz, blend 3 or 4 times, just enough to blend cherries into cheese mixture. Remove mixture to a medium-large mixing bowl.

Toast nuts with sea salt over medium heat in medium-sized frying pan for about 3 minutes turning often until nuts are lightly browned. Remove nuts with slotted spoon. Place half of nuts in small food processor and chop nuts into coarse chopped pieces (pea-sized). Repeat with remainder of nuts.

Add raspberry yogurt to mixture and fold gently. Add chopped nuts and fold gently. Add Grand Marnier liqueur and fold gently. Add Splenda and fold gently. Total preparation time is approximately 20-25 minutes.

Makes 4 cups. Serve on shortbread cookies.

CLING PEACHES, MONTAGUE CHEESE AND ROASTED ALMOND DIP

One of the treats on a trip from the piedmont to the Carolina coast is the drive through the Sandhills during peach season. Roadside stands are filled with cornucopia baskets of the sweetest, juiciest, most succulent peaches one could ever desire. Several little towns such as Ellerbe, North Carolina have roadside stands with homemade peach ice cream that is so sweet, so creamy and soooo good that you don't want to swallow.

The half bushel peach baskets can also double as baby tenders. When my son was about six months old, I would place towels in the bottom of one these baskets, roll towels for bumpers on either side, place diapers at his head and bottles at his feet and strap him in the passenger seat of my sports car. We had fun times at ball games, rodeos and picnics on the riverbank. He doesn't remember these great trips and times afield but I do.

I also have Christmas memories of homemade peach brandy floating atop a cup of Mother's boiled custard creating what the good folk of eastern North Carolina call "selzeeebub" which is an eastern North Carolinaized version of the English word for the dessert selabub.

This dip will rekindle your memories of fresh peaches and treasured summertime experiences.

7 ounces montague cheese
4 ounces cream cheese
Two 4 ounce cups of Yoplait brand Peaches N' Cream low fat yogurt (8 ounces total)
½ pound or ½ jar of Del Monte brand Orchard Select sliced Cling Peaches
4 tablespoons sweet orange marmalade
2 tablespoons Frangelico liqueur
2 tablespoons Grand Marnier liqueur
1 cup whipped cream
1 cup sliced almonds
1 teaspoon sea salt

Grate montague cheese in large food processor. Remove grated cheese from food processor and insert chopping blade. Replace grated cheese in food processor and add cream cheese in thumb-sized pinches. Add yogurt and blend in food processor checking every 15 seconds until you achieve a smooth creamy dip consistency (about 30-45 seconds) that will hold on a thin cookie or wafer. Remove mixture to medium-large mixing bowl.

Remove peaches from syrup with a fork. You do not want to carry syrup to bowl where you are placing peaches. With a small paring knife and a fork, cut peach slices into marble-sized pieces. Add peaches to mixture and fold gently with rubber spatula. Add marmalade and fold gently. Add both liqueurs and fold gently. Add whipped cream and fold gently.

Toast nuts with sea salt over medium heat in medium-sized frying pan for about 3 minutes turning often until nuts are lightly browned. Remove nuts with slotted spoon. Add toasted almond slices to mixture and fold gently. Total preparation time is approximately 20-25 minutes.

Makes 5 cups. Serve on shortbread cookie of choice.

SECTION 5

Desserts and Dessert Dips and Spreads

PUMPKIN, BRANDIED RAISIN AND HAZELNUT DIP

My children loved Halloween, especially my two girls. Carving the pumpkin for their jack-o'-lantern was my treat along with accompanying them in the background as they went about the neighborhood playing trick-or-treat. Each year the carvings became more and more complex. When my younger daughter reached middle school age she no longer wanted to go trick-or-treating, but she still wanted me to sculpt her a pumpkin. By this time in her life the pumpkins required three to four hours per creation. I don't begrudge a minute of this time together. This recipe brings back wonderful memories for me of my children's wonderment, real pumpkin jack-o'-lanterns and the excitement and squeals that accompanied trick-or-treat with my girls.

Mary Elizabeth & Anna's jack-o'-lanterns

One 30 ounce can Libby's brand Easy Pumpkin Pie Mix
⅔ cup condensed milk
3 large eggs (beaten)
8 ounces sharp white cheddar cheese
4 ounces cream cheese
4 heaping teaspoons sour cream
½ cup marshmallow cream
1 cup white raisins (golden)
1 cup water
½ cup hazelnuts
1 teaspoon sea salt
½ ounce Jacques Cardin Napoleon Brandy

Mix can of pumpkin with condensed milk and beaten eggs. Place mixture in uncovered casserole dish. Preheat oven to 425 degrees then reduce to 350 degrees. Place pumpkin mixture in oven at 350 degrees for 1¼ hours or until you can pull a clean knife blade. Let pumpkin cool to room temperature.

Grate white cheddar cheese in food processor. Remove grated cheese from food processor and insert chopping blade. Replace grated cheese in food processor and add cream cheese in teaspoon-sized pinches. Add sour cream, marshmallow cream and blend in food processor checking every 15 seconds until you achieve a smooth creamy dip consistency (about 30-45 seconds) that will hold on a thin cookie or wafer. Place raisins and water in sauce pan. Heat over medium heat until raisins plump. Drain raisins. Medium-coarse chop raisins (until they are almost the size of a whole raisin). Pour Brandy over raisins.

Toast nuts with sea salt over medium heat in medium-sized frying pan for about 3 minutes turning often until nuts are lightly browned. Remove nuts with slotted spoon. To the cheese blend add 15 ounces of the pumpkin mixture and blend. Remove mixture to large mixing bowl. Fold raisins and nuts into cheese mixture with rubber spatula. Total preparation time is approximately 1½ hours including cooling the pumpkin mixture.

Makes 4 cups. Serve on cinnamon graham crackers.

Southerners like their coffee rich, full bodied, dark, strong and with a hint of chicory. Southerners also have a penchant for all that is sweet. If there is a way to make candy or a dessert sweeter and more decadent, the great cooks of the South will find it. Southerners like the taste of chocolate, caramel and toffee.

As a child when my eyes were about to lead my stomach astray and I was given to excess, Papa Hicks would touch me on the shoulder and impart his wisdom, "Tombstone, even homemade ice cream tastes like soap after five bowls." Tombstone was the pet name that he gave to me. He said that we were "tombstone buddies," that's buddies to the grave and we were.

When I conduct a class on gourmet cooking and serve a four course dinner with appropriate wines, I rarely serve a commanding dessert. I generally subscribe to Papa Hicks' admonishment about five bowls or as I would phrase it, less is often more. These meals are generally concluded with a light ramekin-sized dessert and coffee. Occasionally I conclude a meal with a dessert coffee I created which contains the liqueurs in the recipe below. This beverage makes a wonderful ending to a lovely meal and is not heavy. This dips captures that special coffee and transforms it into a spreadable form. It is decadent.

5 ounces sharp white cheddar cheese
1 cup plain non-fat yogurt
8 ounces cream cheese
$\frac{1}{2}$ cup marshmallow cream
1 tablespoon Bailey's Original Irish Cream liqueur
1 tablespoon Arrow Creme de Cacao dark liqueur
1 tablespoon Kahlúa liqueur
2 tablespoons Frangelico liqueur
5 tablespoons Britt Licor de Cafe coffee liqueur
2 ounces chocolate-covered coffee beans
1 tablespoon medium ground French Roast coffee
One 1.4 ounce Heath English Toffee Bar
10 packages Splenda brand sweetener
1 + cups whipped cream

Grate white cheddar cheese in large food processor. Remove grated cheese from food processor and insert chopping blade. Replace grated cheese in food processor and add cream cheese in pinches. Add yogurt and blend. Add marshmallow cream and blend. Check every 15 seconds as you blend. You want a smooth creamy dip consistency (approximately 30-45 seconds total blending time) that will hold on a thin cookie or wafer. Remove mixture to medium-large mixing bowl. Add Creme de Cacao dark, Bailey's, Kahlúa and Britt Licor de Café. Fold gently.

Place 1 ounce of chocolate-covered coffee beans in small food processor. Blend on high until medium-coarse. Do not pulverize. Add to mixture. Repeat with remaining chocolate-covered coffee beans and fold. Add Frangelico and fold. Add ground coffee to mixture and fold gently.

Break and cut Health Bar into small pieces (nickel-sized) and place into small food processor. Buzz on high. Do not make candy into meal. You want small nugget pieces for crumbs. Add Heath Bar to mixture and fold gently.

Add Spenda to mixture and fold gently. Add 1 cup whipped cream and fold gently. Add more whipped cream if you want a thicker dip.

I suggest you taste this dip as you move along. If you want a stronger coffee presence add more coffee. Taste before adding the Splenda. Add Spenda two packets at a time and fold. Tastes differ on coffee strength, sweetness, etc. just as people prefer their coffee in different ways. Total preparation time is approximately 35-40 minutes. Makes 4 cups. Serve on sugar cookies or Daelman's Caramel Bites.

SWEET POTATO, COCONUT AND
TOASTED PECAN PRALINE DIP

$\mathcal{M}$ost of my father's family, the Early's, in my opinion, seemed to view food as fuel to be taken on as replenishment in order to enable one to continue working. My mother's family, the Hicks, viewed eating as a celebration. Only the slightest provocation could produce a celebration, "Have you had a good day?" "You have!" "Well Lord child, let's cook a pig, make a brunswick stew or turn a freezer of cream."

The Hicks were big on reunions. They were held at Island Creek Baptist Church just outside of Hicksboro which was settled by the Hicks' family. All the Hicks that had gone to a larger table were buried there. I remember the feasts prepared by my mother's aunts and my mother's generation of great country cooks. Sadly the fare at reunions of late has not been free range chicken, fried in a black iron skillet with fatback drippings, but rather its city cousin removed from a cardboard bucket. Forget butterbeans cooked with country ham or side meat, and a homemade from-scratch dessert is a rarity.

Island Creek Baptist Church, circa 1800s

As I grow longer of tooth I realize that the gathering and the fellowship are more important than the food. However, my mind often wanders to a kinder, gentler time when the food was prepared by weathered hands with a loving touch and perhaps just a little competitive one-ups-manship. On those occasions everyone always saved a place on their plate for Aunt Pearl's grated sweet potato pudding. Despite an array of wonderful desserts made by the best country cooks in the county, I always chose seconds on Aunt Pearl's sweet potato pudding over the cakes, pies, banana puddings, etc. This recipe captures the flavor of that wonderful concoction that only Aunt Pearl could do so well.

One 15 ounce can S&W brand candied yams
¼ stick salted butter
½ cup medium chopped fresh coconut
½ cup marshmallow cream
4 heaping teaspoons sour cream
½ cup dark raisins
1 cup water
1 teaspoon Jacques Cardin Napoleon Brandy
½ cup pecans
1 teaspoon sugar
8 ounces sharp white cheddar cheese
4 ounces cream cheese
1 teaspoon sea salt
2 sprays butter flavored cooking spray

Cook sweet potatoes in covered dish in 350 degree oven for 20 minutes. Drain potatoes and save juice. Purée hot potatoes with butter. Grate white cheddar cheese in large food processor. Remove grated cheese from food processor and insert chopping blade. Replace grated cheese in food processor and add cream cheese in teaspoon-sized pinches. Add sour cream, 2 teaspoons of the sweet potato juices and blend. Add sweet potatoes to cheese mixture and blend. Add marshmallow cream and blend. Add coconut and buzz enough to just mix. Check as you blend. You want a smooth creamy dip consistency that will hold on a thin cookie or wafer (about 30-45 seconds total blending time).

Cook raisins in water until raisins plump (About 4-5 minutes at medium heat). Drain raisins and coarse chop (about ½ raisin size). Pour Brandy over raisins.

Toast nuts with sea salt over medium heat in medium-sized frying pan for about 3 minutes turning often until nuts are lightly browned. Remove nuts with slotted spoon. Dump salt in trash. Replace nuts in frying pan and spray lightly with butter spray. Add sugar to pecans and toss in pan until coated. Warm nuts for 1 or 2 minutes but do not brown nuts or cook nuts. Remove nuts with slotted spoon. Chop pecans medium-coarse.

Fold pecan pieces and raisins into sweet potato mixture. Add 2 teaspoons sweet potato juice if needed to obtain a dip texture. Add 1 teaspoon at a time. You do not want the dip to be runny. It should have a nice soft texture that is easy to dip and will stay on a cookie. Total preparation time is approximately 40 minutes.

Makes 4-5 cups. Serve on ginger snap cookies.

KEY LIME AND
PISTACHIO NUT DIP

One of my favorite fishing holes is Islamorada Key, Florida. I enjoy fishing out of Bud and Mary's Marina. About two-thirds the distance from Bud & Mary's to my favorite sand box, Key West, is a small island called Sugarloaf Key. There is a restaurant on this island that has traditionally made some of the best key lime pie that I have ever tasted. It is pound-the-table and write-a-postcard-home good. My goal with this recipe was to capture the rich, creamy, tartness and sweetness of that memorable dessert in the form of a dip. Tweak the recipe with lime curd or condensed milk to your particular taste and memory of the best key lime pie that you've ever had and share.

First light, Islamorada Key, Florida

5 ounces sharp white cheddar cheese
4 ounces cream cheese
1 package Sans Sucre brand key lime pie filling
1 cup half & half milk
Two 6 ounce cups of Yoplait brand custard style key lime pie yogurt (12 ounces)
10 + tablespoons sweetened condensed milk
2 fresh key limes
½ cup pistachio nuts
1 + tablespoons lime curd

Grate white cheddar cheese in large food processor. Remove grated cheese from food processor and insert chopping blade. Replace grated cheese in food processor and add cream cheese in thumb-sized pinches. Add yogurt and blend for about 30 seconds.

Place pie filling in a food processor with chopping blade inserted. Add half & half milk and blend slowly for 1 minute. Blend medium for 2 minutes. Add pie mixture to cheese mixture and blend. Check as you blend. You wish to have a smooth creamy dip consistency that will hold on a thin cookie or wafer. Remove to medium-large mixing bowl. Add 10 tablespoons condensed milk to mixture and fold with rubber spatula

Quarter 1 lime. Squeeze juice into mixture and fold. Repeat with second lime. Take the second lime and slice into ¼ inch pieces cut lengthwise. Place 2 or 3 pieces of sliced lime into small food processor and buzz on high speed until you have small (¼ Rice Crispy size) pieces. Repeat with the rest of the lime slices. This should produce about 2 - 2½ tablespoons of ground lime peel and pulp. Add ground lime to mixture and fold.

Place pistachio nuts in small food processor and buzz on high speed until nuts are approximately half of whole size. Add nuts to mixture and fold gently. To increase tartness, add lime curd 1 tablespoon at a time to reach desired taste. To make sweeter, add more condensed milk 1 tablespoon at a time to reach desired taste. Total preparation time is approximately 30-35 minutes.

Makes 3½ cups. Serve on graham crackers.

At Hicks' family gatherings, while the women talked in the "sitting parlor" the men quietly drifted to the kitchen where they knew Aunt Pearl's cupboard contained at least one quart of homemade fruit brandy. At Christmas Aunt Pearl would wrap her fruitcakes in cheese cloth and moisten the cloth with brandy to keep her cakes from drying during the holiday season. For the men of the Hicks' clan a teaspoon floater of brandy on a cup of hot boiled custard transformed what the Brits called selabub into a dish that rural folk in eastern North Carolina call "selzeeebub."

One of my favorite "selzeeebub" stories occurred when a long standing client of mine who hunted deer the week before Christmas in the mountains and the week after Christmas in the Sandhills ran into the long arms of the law. While hunting in the mountains my client was lucky enough to successfully take a large buck at twilight. My client was laboring to drag his trophy to his truck which was a good piece away when he ran into an old mountain man whose truck was parked near by. The mountain man helped my client drag the deer to his vehicle and transported my client and the deer to my client's truck. Then in the spirit of Christmas the mountain man invited my client to supper. My client accepted and in the same spirit gave the mountain man a hind quarter off of his deer. Continuing the spirit of giving the mountain man gave my client a quart of homemade peach brandy. After Christmas my client, while on his way to the Sandhills, had the misfortune of having a man in a $150.00 car run a stop sign and hit his new automobile, abandon the car and run from the scene. My client called the police who investigated. When questioned about whether there was any alcohol involved and did he have any in the car, my client opened the trunk to show the officer a fifth of whiskey with the seal unbroken. In rummaging through the box of goodies, the officer discovered the quart of homemade brandy which my client was taking to his host in the Sandhills. Ooops!

The officer promptly took my client into custody, impounded the car and all of my client's hunting paraphernalia. On Saturday night as I was about to serve dessert at a dinner party that I had prepared for friends, I received the call. Help! I excused myself and drove to the neighboring city and spent the next three hours trying to arrange bail and extract my client from the jaws of justice and the enthusiasm of a young officer who seemed convinced that he had caught Al Capone's counterpart in North Carolina.

On the day of trial I had the good fortune to draw, as a trial judge, a newly appointed female judge, who prior to going on the bench acquired a vast knowledge of alcohol and alcohol related events in her criminal practice. I recited to the judge the deer hunting story and how my client came to possess the quart of homemade peach brandy. I also informed the judge of my client's intent to further gift the brandy to his old friend and host in the Sandhills of our state. I shared with the judge that I was born in eastern North Carolina and all of my aunts were God fearing, church going Christian women and that to my knowledge most of them possessed at least one quart of good homemade brandy used to wrap their fruitcakes and for medicinal purposes. I explained to the judge that a cup of good homemade boiled custard with a teaspoon of brandy was called "selzeeebub." I further explained that "selzeeebub" was as much a part of Christmas in eastern North Carolina as Santa Claus.

The judge smiled kindly and shared that she was familiar with the customs of eastern North Carolina and had had the privilege of partaking of "selzeeebub." She further inquired that if she amended the warrant from possession of illegal non tax paid whiskey with intent to sell to read that my client was in possession of one quart of good homemade brandy, and that she would underline good, did I think that my client would be willing to pay court costs (about $25.00). I quickly advised the court that my client would pay costs all the while suppressing the urge to kneel and kiss the hem of her robe.

4 quarts half & half milk
12 tablespoons (level) cornstarch
4¼ cups white sugar
16 eggs
4 teaspoons vanilla extract
1 pinch of salt

Separate the whites and yolks of 6 eggs. Set the 6 egg whites aside and save if you are going to make the banana pudding recipe on the next page, Cousin Leigh's birthday cake or seafoam candy with pecans, if not then discard the 6 egg whites. In a large bowl combine your dry ingredients, cornstarch, sugar and salt together. In another large bowl whisk your 10 whole eggs and the yolks from 6 eggs until the mixture is well blended. Continuing to stir, pour in half & half milk. Then continuing to stir, add dry ingredients at point of stirring to prevent lumps. When your liquid is satin smooth, pour into double boiler and cook, uncovered over hot almost boiling water stirring occasionally until your custard begins to thicken. If you are making the custard as a stand alone, cook for approximately 30-35 minutes or until it will coat a wooden spoon. If you are making this custard for the banana pudding on the next page, you may wish to cook for approximately 30-32 minutes so the custard can get down into the bananas and wafers. Remove from heat and add vanilla extract. Set custard aside to cool.

To make "selzeeebub" simply serve custard medium to hot in a mug. Make a cross (x) with homemade fruit brandy – peach, apricot and apple are all good. I suggest ½ to 1 teaspoon (to taste).

This custard can also be served as sweet cream with raspberries or other fresh fruit layered in a small parfait glass without liqueur (if preferred). Add a dollop of real whipped cream on top.

Total preparation time is approximately 40-45 minutes.
Makes 4 quarts.

*U*ntil the time of her death in 1984 my mother made fantastic banana pudding. Mother's recipe was handed down from her mother who received it from her mother. In fact I think all of the Hicks' women use pretty much the same recipe for this Southern dish.

I read cookbooks like most people read newspapers. In the 100 plus banana pudding recipes I have encountered in my reading, I have seen only miniscule variance and pretty much the same ingredients in the recipes proffered by each cook. I have taken my mother's banana pudding recipe up about four clicks. To me the secret of a good banana pudding is first having a great made-from-scratch boiled custard as opposed to instant puddings, etc. The second is to have good ripe bananas with lot of freckles and brown streaks. Most bananas sold at grocery stores and "fresh markets" are too green for good banana pudding. The only other ingredient is vanilla wafers. I am fond of Nilla brand wafers.

When I am constructing a banana pudding I pour my custard hot over the bananas and wafers. I make my meringue with egg whites and sugar, sprinkling enough cream of tarter as I mix the meringue to achieve the form of peaks I desire. I do not like a particularly "stiff" meringue. I prefer a thicker meringue topping with softer peaks spread to completely cover the custard surface so that it does not separate from the wafer edge.

The boiled custard recipe on the previous page is the custard recipe used as the base for this banana pudding. I cook the boiled custard four or five minutes less for banana pudding than the cooking time called for if I am serving the custard as a stand alone. I like my hot custard for this recipe to be a little more runny so it can reach every nook and cranny and can be more easily absorbed by the wafers in the body of the pudding.

I prefer to make my banana pudding at least one day prior to serving it as a dessert. This allows the custard, bananas and wafers to get to know one another. To refrigerate I place six or eight toothpicks strategically in the meringue to hold the aluminum foil cover off of the meringue and protect the peaks. This creates a nice tent and will allow your meringue to still look pretty when you remove the foil and the toothpicks.

Make ¼ of the boiled custard on previous recipe. Cook the custard approximately 30-32 minutes
6 egg whites
4-6 fully ripe, firm bananas, sliced across the banana
1 box Nabisco brand Nilla Wafers
¼ cup sugar
½ teaspoon cream of tarter

Line bottom and sides of a 9 inch by 13 inch or larger baking dish with Nilla wafers. Arrange wafers around the sides of dish so that half of wafer extends above edge of dish. Cover the bottom layer of Nilla wafers with sliced bananas. Pour a small amount of custard over your first layer of wafers and bananas and repeat until the dish is full with the top layer being custard. Do not fill to the top but allow approximately ½ inch for meringue.

In a separate bowl whisk the 6 egg whites, stiff but not dry. Add sugar as you whisk and continue to whisk until mixture forms stiff peaks. Add sprinkles of cream of tarter to promote stiffening of meringue as you mix. I prefer an electric mixer equipped with a whisk. Spread meringue on top of pudding covering entire top to each edge. Bake in preheated oven (425 degrees) for 5 minutes or until light golden brown.

Set pudding aside to cool for several hours and allow the Nilla wafers, bananas and custard to get to know one another. If the pudding is not to be eaten within 4-5 hours of completing, place toothpicks in the pudding to support aluminum foil, cover completely and refrigerate.

When serving later, the pudding does not have to be reheated but simply brought out and allowed to rest at room temperature for an hour or so before serving. Serves 12-15.

Total preparation time is approximately 1 hour.

BETTER THAN SEX CHOCOLATE PIE

Still searching for other places to take my new creation of Mama Hicks' Chocolate Pie, I decided that since Papa Hicks liked her pie so well with dark coffee with chicory that I would arrange a marriage for the two.

In this recipe I wanted to maintain the integrity of the wonderful chocolate flavor that is Mama Hicks' Chocolate Pie and bring about a new union with a good coffee flavor, thus achieving the best taste of both worlds. To achieve this taste I first concocted Mama Hicks original chocolate pie filling and added Frangelico liqueur, Britt Licor de Café coffee liqueur, ground hazelnut coffee (unbrewed), dark chocolate-covered espresso beans and milk chocolate-covered espresso beans.

The title of this pie was bestowed by one of the ladies at the little diner where I often take lunch. Since there is great variance in each person's appetites, personal life and penchant for chocolate, I made no inquiry as to where her sex life and her taste for chocolate fit on a scale of 1-10. I simply acknowledged her compliment of my creation and named the pie accordingly. However, if you find yourself tugged toward eating this pie rather than having great sex, I think you may wish to consider serious counseling.

One 9 inch deep dish frozen pie shell (thawed)
$\frac{1}{4}$ pound salted butter
2 squares unsweetened chocolate
2 eggs
1 cup sugar
$\frac{1}{4}$ cup flour
$\frac{1}{4}$ teaspoon salt
1 teaspoon vanilla
3 tablespoons Frangelico liqueur
3 tablespoons Britt Licor de Cafe coffee liqueur
4 tablespoons freshly ground hazelnut coffee (unbrewed)
$\frac{1}{4}$ cup dark chocolate-covered espresso beans
$\frac{1}{4}$ cup milk chocolate-covered espresso beans

Squeeze the dough around the edge of pie shell between your thumb and forefinger and pinch scallops so your pie shell will look like a homemade pie shell and not a commercial product. Set pie shell aside.

Place butter and chocolate in a medium mixing bowl and microwave for approximately 3 minutes until the butter and the chocolate are melted. Fold butter and chocolate. In a large mixing bowl add eggs and sugar and blend well with a whisk. Add chocolate butter mixture to eggs and blend. Add vanilla, flour and salt to mixture and continue blending. Add liqueurs and fold.

Place the dark chocolate-covered espresso beans in a sandwich bag and zip. Place the sandwich bag on a chopping block to protect your countertop and lightly smash the beans with a hammer. Do not powder the beans, simply reduce them to pieces the size of Rice Crispies or half of a Rice Crispy. Repeat this procedure with the milk chocolate-covered espresso beans. Add the smashed beans to mixture and fold with a rubber spatula. Add the hazelnut coffee to mixture and fold with a rubber spatula.

When mixture is well blended, pour the mixture into unbaked and thawed pie shell. Cut strips of aluminum foil the width of the roll and approximately 3 inches wide. Crimp the aluminum foil under the aluminum pie dish holding your pie shell. Gently make a canopy over the exposed pie crust. This will prevent the pie crust from browning and will give a nicer appearance to your pie.

Bake pie in a preheated oven at 350 degrees for approximately 47-49 minutes. Check middle of pie with a toothpick. If the toothpick pulls out clean, your pie is ready. If the toothpick has particles of batter on it, continue to bake pie checking every 1-2 minutes.

Remove pie from oven and place on rack to cool. Cut pie with a wet sharp knife cleaned after each slice to reduce drag. A small sliver of this pie is sufficient for dessert as it is quite rich. Garnish each slice of pie with a dollop of real whipped cream, mint leaves and a dark chocolate-covered espresso bean.

Total preparation time is approximately 1¼ hours.

"THE BOMB" CARAMEL CAKE

Aunt Pearl and Mary Elizabeth

*I*n the South I would suspect that everybody's granny had a version of a caramel cake. These rich wonderful concoctions were Southern grannies' benchmark expression of love. These cakes were served at celebrations, reunions, birthdays, to soothe hurt feelings and heal skinned knees. It was almost worth losing a little hide to hear the words, "Bless your heart child, sit on this stool and I'll make you a caramel cake."

Though my Aunt Pearl never had any children of her own, I was the lucky one that she "adopted." I was fortunate to be able to spend a lot of time at the Hicks' home place with Aunt Pearl. I "helped" her cook, do dishes, set tables, gather eggs, tote wood, churn butter, slop hogs, tend garden and in season handed her leaves when she was stringing tobacco.

Somehow in the course of a week of "helping with chores" I was able to find an old gate, a rock or stick of wood that produced the pinch, the bruise or the splinter that merited a caramel cake. I will never forget the acts of kindness and love from this wonderful woman to a red-headed, freckle-faced cowboy who thought that a week at Aunt Pearl's was second only to heaven, and that surely she was God's favorite angel.

The following is my attempt to duplicate Aunt Pearl's caramel cake. When you or someone you love has a "hurt," this cake is the "bestest band aid."

For your cake layers you can use the from-scratch recipe below or use 1 box of your favorite yellow cake mix and cook per instructions listed on the back of the box.

FROM-SCRATCH CAKE LAYERS

3½ cups all purpose flour
1 teaspoon baking powder
1 cup milk
2 teaspoons vanilla
3 eggs
1½ cups vegetable oil
2 cups sugar
1 pinch salt

Preheat oven to 375 degrees or 350 degrees if using dark cake pans. Prepare 3 cake pans by lightly greasing the inside of each pan with shortening. Then cut wax paper to fit the inside bottom of the pans and line the inside bottom of the pans with the wax paper to keep your cake bottoms from burning. Next grease the wax paper with shortening. The goal here is to achieve a lightly greased wax paper. Do not over-grease. Sprinkle flour in the greased cake pans on the bottom and sides. Shake the cake pans to achieve a light flour coating (i.e. dusting) on sides and bottom. Dump excess flour in trash and set cake pans aside.

Sift about 3½ cups of flour into a medium-sized mixing bowl. Remeasure flour and retain 3 sifted leveled cups in mixing bowl. Dump excess flour. Add baking powder and salt, lightly blend with a whisk and set aside. In a second bowl add milk and vanilla, stir and set aside.

Into a large mixing bowl place sugar and vegetable oil and mix with electric mixer for about 2 minutes until well blended. Add 1 whole egg to the sugar and oil mixture and blend with electric mixer at medium speed for 2 minutes. Repeat this process with each of your three eggs. Next add 1 cup of your dry ingredients to oil and sugar mixture. Beat with electric mixer at low speed for approximately 2 minutes (only enough to blend). Add half of your milk to this mixture and beat for 2 minutes (only enough to blend). Next add 1 cup of your dry mixture and beat for 2 minutes (only enough to blend). Add the remainder of your milk and beat for 2 minutes (only enough to blend). Add the remainder of your dry mixture and beat for 2 minutes (only enough to blend). Do not over-mix. You should have a smooth mixture that is slightly thicker than pancake batter and will pour easily.

Divide batter into 3 prepared cake pans. Bump the bottom of the cake pans on a countertop several times to seat batter. This helps prevent doming of the cake layers. Place cake pans in preheated oven and bake for approximately 20-23 minutes. Check middle of layers with a toothpick. If the toothpick pulls out clean, your layers are ready. If the toothpick has particles of batter on it, continue to bake layers checking every 1-2 minutes. Cooking times will vary depending upon your oven. Allow cake layers to cool for at least 10 minutes before removing from pan onto cooling rack or plates

Place your hand over the layer, turn pan upside down, thump the pan on the bottom and your layer should drop. Set your baking tin aside, place your free hand on the bottom of the cake, turn layer over and place to rest on cooling rack or plate. If your layers have domed, save the layer with the smallest dome for your top layer, take a long bread knife and slice horizontally to remove the dome from the bottom 2 layers so that they are flat. Place your bottom layer on the plate chosen for your cake. The plate should be sufficiently larger than the cake to permit icing of the cake without the icing flowing over the plate. A flat plate is preferred to one with a lip. Do not use a plate with an indented center.

For a more moist cake layer see *Tips for Cooking* section of this book.

CARAMEL ICING

2 pounds brown sugar (5 cups)
1 pound white sugar (2$\frac{1}{2}$ cups)
$\frac{1}{2}$ stick salted butter
2$\frac{1}{4}$ cups half & half milk
$\frac{1}{4}$ cup white corn syrup
3 tablespoons Basilica Hazelnut liqueur
1 tablespoon Bailey's Original Irish Cream liqueur
2 tablespoons Britt Licor de Cafe coffee liqueur

Place the first 5 icing ingredients together in a cooking pot large enough to hold the ingredients and not be more than half full. This is to allow for boiling with minimal splattering. Start with a cold cooking surface. Set stove at medium-high and cook and stir ingredients until ingredients form into a soft ball. The mixture should boil at approximately 8 minutes. Cook at a boil stirring for 7 more minutes. Total cooking time is approximately 15 minutes. Remove icing from heat and pour into a large mixing bowl. Add liqueurs. Beat icing mixture 13-15 minutes on high. Check consistency each minute beginning at 12 minutes. At approximately 13 minutes icing should be thick enough to spread without running off of layers. Be attentive and do not over-beat. Icing will continue to cool and harden. Do not make your icing ahead of time. Make only after your cake layers have cooled and been cut (if necessary) as the icing will become too thick to spread. If your icing becomes too thick to spread easily, add half & half milk 1 tablespoon at a time and soften your icing to desired consistency.

  Have several glasses of hot water and 3-4 wide blade dinner knives for spreading. Spread a fairly generous amount of icing evenly on top of bottom layer. Wet knife between each spreading so as not to pull cake layer into your icing due to drag. Work quickly. Next place middle layer on top of the bottom layer. Repeat icing process with middle layer. Next seat the top layer (the smallest domed of the layers). Ice top layer and sides of cake working quickly. Wet and use a clean knife as much as possible as this icing is tacky and tends to pull. You need to work quickly with caramel icing. It will cool, harden and be difficult to spread much sooner than other icings. After you have completely iced the cake you are ready to decorate in any manner you choose.

  Total cooking, cooling and icing time is approximately 2 + hours

The three years that I taught gourmet cooking classes at Salem College in Winston-Salem, North Carolina, I often used a special coffee in lieu of dessert. After a four course pheasant dinner with appropriate wines, etc. most of my class was not in the mood for a heavy dessert. On these occasions I often used a very light and small dessert or a dessert coffee I concocted called "Jim's Joe."

Jim's Joe is made by placing half of a Heath Bar in the bottom of an Irish whiskey mug and adding freshly ground and freshly brewed dark coffee, filling approximately half the mug. Then add equal parts Bailey's Original Irish Cream, Kahlúa and Arrow Creme de Cacao dark liqueurs. The mixture is then placed in the microwave for approximately 20 seconds to raise the heat of the coffee after adding the liqueurs. It is intended that the drink be served hot. This offering was then topped with real whipped cream, sprinkled with Frangelico liqueur and garnished with shaved sweet chocolate or Heath Bar pieces. Add a straw and wallah – Jim's Joe!

This chocolate pie recipe captures all of the rich brownie qualities of Mama Hicks' Chocolate Pie and takes it to another level with the additions of the liqueurs and toasted pecans. I hope you will enjoy this pie as well.

One 9 inch deep dish frozen pie shell (thawed)
¼ pound salted butter
2 squares unsweetened chocolate
2 eggs
1 cup sugar
¼ cup flour
¼ teaspoon salt
1 teaspoon vanilla
2 tablespoons Bailey's Original Irish Cream liqueur
2 tablespoons Kahlúa liqueur
2 tablespoons Arrow Creme de Cacao dark liqueur
½ cup medium chopped pecan pieces
½ tablespoon sea salt

Squeeze the dough around the edge of pie shell between your thumb and forefinger and pinch scallops so your pie shell will look like a homemade pie shell and not a commercial product. Set pie shell aside.

Place butter and chocolate in a medium mixing bowl and microwave for approximately 3 minutes until the butter and the chocolate are melted. Fold butter and chocolate. In a large mixing bowl add eggs and sugar and blend well with a whisk. Add chocolate butter mixture to eggs and blend. Add vanilla, flour, liqueurs and salt to mixture and continue blending.

Place pecan pieces in small fry pan on medium heat and sprinkle with sea salt. Heat pecan pieces over medium heat turning with a spoon to expose pecan pieces to the salt. This should take about 3 minutes. Remove pecan pieces with a slotted spoon. Dump salt in trash. Add the pecan pieces to your pie mixture as your last ingredient and fold evenly with a rubber spatula.

When mixture is well blended, pour the mixture into your unbaked and thawed pie shell. Cut strips of aluminum foil the width of the roll and approximately 3 inches wide. Crimp the aluminum foil under the aluminum pie dish holding your pie shell. Gently make a canopy over the exposed pie crust. This will prevent the pie crust from browning and will give a nicer appearance to your pie.

Bake pie in a preheated oven at 350 degrees for approximately 47-49 minutes. Check middle of pie with a toothpick. If the toothpick pulls out clean, your pie is ready. If the toothpick has particles of batter on it, continue to bake pie checking every 1-2 minutes.

Remove pie from oven and place on rack to cool. Cut pie with a wet sharp knife cleaned after each slice to reduce drag. A small sliver of this pie is sufficient for dessert as it is quite rich.

Total preparation time is approximately 1 hour.

COUSIN LEIGH'S BIRTHDAY CAKE

*M*y favorite cousin is Leigh Hicks Finch. Leigh is the quintessential "Queen Bee." I consider myself a wordsmith but I am at a loss to describe the lengths to which people have gone, and to this day continue to go, to spoil this woman. Leigh was the high school queen, the college bell of the ball and the apple of everyone's eye since birth. The wonderful thing about Leigh is, with no expectations, she spoils her family and friends as much or more than they happily seek to spoil her.

Leigh, now 75 years young, is still as cute as a button, vivacious and as squeezable as she was at age 15. She still sings and plays the piano by ear like everyone else wishes they could. When Leigh plays Pinetop Smith's Boogie Woogie (a.k.a Tommy Dorsey's Boogie Woogie) on the piano, she rocks the house. As are most of the Hicks' women (especially of Leigh's vintage), Leigh is an excellent country cook. However, on her birthday it was Leigh's annual request that Aunt Pearl make her one of Aunt Pearl's special desserts, an offering Aunt Pearl called a Lady Baltimore cake. At the tender age of 5 years I "helped" Aunt Pearl make this cake. At this writing with the assistance of Hicks' women I was able to pick up enough threads to weave a baseline cake that closely resembled Aunt Pearl's mouthwatering concoction. From this launch pad I attempted to soar and create a new and better offering.

Leigh, here is your cake.

For your cake layers you can use the from-scratch recipe below or use 1 box of your favorite yellow cake mix and cook per instructions listed on the back of the box. See *Tips for Cooking* section.

*Leigh Hicks Finch
and the Cowboy*

FROM-SCRATCH CAKE LAYERS

3½ cups all purpose flour
1 teaspoon baking powder
1 cup milk
2 teaspoons vanilla
3 eggs
1½ cups vegetable oil
2 cups sugar
1 pinch salt
9 tablespoons coconut milk or pineapple juice or combination thereof (to
    drizzle on cake layers)

Preheat oven to 375 degrees or 350 degrees if using dark cake pans. Prepare 3 cake pans by lightly greasing the inside of each pan with shortening. Then cut wax paper to fit the inside bottom of the pans and line the inside bottom of the pans with the wax paper to keep your cake bottoms from burning. Next grease the wax paper with shortening. The goal here is to achieve a lightly greased wax paper. Do not over-grease. Sprinkle flour in the greased cake pans on the bottom and sides. Shake the cake pans to achieve a light flour coating (i.e. dusting) on sides and bottom. Dump excess flour in trash and set cake pans aside.

Sift about 3½ cups of flour into a medium-sized mixing bowl. Remeasure flour and retain 3 sifted leveled cups in mixing bowl. Dump excess flour. Add baking powder and salt, lightly blend with a whisk and set aside. In a second bowl add milk and vanilla, stir and set aside.

Into a large mixing bowl place sugar and vegetable oil and mix with electric mixer for about 2 minutes until well blended. Add 1 whole egg to the sugar and oil mixture and blend with electric mixer at medium speed for 2 minutes. Repeat this process with each of your three eggs. Next add 1 cup of your dry ingredients to oil and sugar mixture. Beat with electric mixer at low speed for approximately 2 minutes (only enough to blend). Add half of your milk to this mixture and beat for 2 minutes (only enough to blend). Next add 1 cup of your dry mixture and beat for 2 minutes (only enough to blend). Add the remainder of your milk and beat for 2 minutes (only enough to blend). Add the remainder of your dry mixture and beat for 2 minutes (only enough to blend). Do not over-mix. You should have a smooth mixture that is slightly thicker than pancake batter and will pour easily.

Divide batter into 3 prepared cake pans. Bump the bottom of the cake pans on a countertop several times to seat batter. This helps prevent doming of the cake layers. Place cake pans in preheated oven and bake for approximately 20-23 minutes. Check middle of layers with a toothpick. If the toothpick pulls out clean, your layers are ready. If the toothpick has particles of batter on it, continue to bake layers checking every 1-2 minutes. Cooking times will vary depending upon your oven. Allow cake layers to cool for at least 10 minutes before removing from pan onto cooling rack or plates

Place your hand over the layer, turn pan upside down, thump the pan on the bottom and your layer should drop. Set your baking tin aside, place your free hand on the bottom of the cake, turn layer over and place to rest on cooling rack or plate. If your layers have domed, save the layer with the smallest dome for your top layer, take a long bread knife and slice horizontally to remove the dome from the bottom 2 layers so that they are flat. Place your bottom layer on the plate chosen for your cake. The plate should be sufficiently larger than the cake to permit icing of the cake without the icing flowing over the plate. A flat plate is preferred to one with a lip. Do not use a plate with an indented center.

With a dinner fork punch a number of holes in the tops of your cake layers that you did not have to remove domes. Then drizzle 3 tablespoons of pineapple juice/coconut milk over each layer 1 tablespoon at a time. Drizzle juice slowly so that it will seep into the holes and not run off layers.

ICING

4 cups sugar
1³/₄ cups water
1 pinch salt
³/₄ teaspoon cream of tarter
3 egg whites
³/₄ teaspoon vanilla
¹/₂ cup whole English walnuts
¹/₂ cup coarse chopped English walnuts

Combine first 3 ingredients in a 2 quart sauce pan, place on cold stove eye and set stove to medium-low heat (on my electric stove this is number 4). Cook mixture stirring occasionally. The mixture should cook at a simmer or bubble but not a hard boil. Cook your mixture until it cooks down to a point that it will spin a thread. A thread is an approximately 2 inch thin thread of syrup when the syrup is gently poured from the edge of a spoon. The total cooking time takes approximately 45-50 minutes. The last 5 minutes are critical and the mixture should be checked every 10-15 seconds. Before the mixture has cooked 30 minutes, beat egg whites with electric mixer with whisk attachment. When whites begin to stiffen, add cream of tartar and continue to mix until whites form stiff peaks. Change electric mixer to regular beating attachments and have vanilla ready to be added to water and sugar mixture.

When the water and sugar mixture forms a thread, immediately remove from heat. Slowly pour hot sugar mixture over egg whites while continuing to beat egg whites with electric mixer at high speed. Add vanilla to your mixture and continue to beat for 8-9 minutes. This should produce a thick creamy mixture that will spread with a knife.

Have several glasses of hot water and 3-4 wide blade dinner knives for spreading. Spread a fairly generous amount of icing evenly on top of bottom layer. Wet knife between each spreading so as not to pull cake layer into your icing due to drag. Work quickly. Next place middle layer on top of the bottom layer. Repeat icing process with middle layer. Next seat the top layer (the smallest domed of the layers). Ice top layer and sides of cake working quickly. Wet and use a clean knife as much as possible as this icing is tacky and tends to pull.

Decorate the top of your cake with whole walnuts in a design of your choice. Sprinkle chopped walnuts between the whole walnuts on top of cake. Place chopped walnuts around the sides of your cake. Let cake rest until icing sets. The icing should take on a firm creamy texture and allow for cutting after several hours. Cut cake with a clean wet knife to produce clean cuts. Total cooking, cooling and icing time is approximately 2 + hours.

My great Uncle Frank Hicks lived in Hicksboro at Hicks' Crossroads, about 10 miles from town (Henderson, North Carolina). Uncle Frank and his wife Aunt Irma lived in a lovely farmhouse surrounded by big trees, a barn, a corn crib, chicken house and other outbuildings. Three things stand out in my mind about a visit to their home: (1) Getting to ride Buck, a dapple gray mule who refused to pull a tobacco slide. (2) Listening to their daughter Leigh play the piano. (3) "Helping" Aunt Irma make her wonderful coconut pie.

Spending time with Uncle Frank and Aunt Irma provided more opportunities to have fun and get into trouble than one could condense into three volumes. Everyday was a so-much-to-do and so-little-time. I have always heard it said, "God watches over drunks and children." I know this is true for the latter group. If it were not so, many of us would not be here today. A week's visit by this cowboy to Uncle Frank's farm at age ten certainly was a 24/7 test of this theory.

The author and Buck

On one visit I discovered in a corral a steer which had, unbeknownst to me, been corn fed for weeks to ready it for market. About the same time I discovered a new plow line hanging on a peg. I fashioned a lasso and proceeded to spend the balance of the afternoon chasing, roping and releasing this steer. The steer and I ran out of gas about the same time, called it a day and I went to the house. Sometime later I was informed that the steer had to be fattened for several more weeks to again ready it for market. I am sure the steer was pleased with his reprieve. Uncle Frank managed to mask his feelings about the matter. Thankfully Aunt Irma intervened on my behalf and I too got a stay of execution.

I know a coconut pie does not generally consort with flaming cherries jubilee or an exquisite torte, but if you wish to treat someone special to a simple offering that is "killer," this is the one. Below is Aunt Irma's coconut pie recipe plus some "goodies" I thought were a good fit. Crank up the coffee pot.

One 9 inch deep dish frozen pie shell (thawed)
1 cup sugar
2 eggs
1 stick melted salted butter
³/₄ cup half & half milk
³/₄ cup fresh shredded coconut or 6 ounce package frozen shredded coconut
¹/₂ teaspoon vanilla
¹/₂ tablespoon Basilica Hazelnut liqueur
¹/₂ tablespoon Frangelico liqueur
¹/₃ cup chopped almonds
¹/₃ cup white chocolate morsels

Squeeze the dough around the edge of pie shell between your thumb and forefinger and pinch scallops so pie shell will look like a homemade pie shell and not a commercial product. Set pie shell aside.

Mix all ingredients well and pour the mixture into your pie shell. Cut strips of aluminum foil the width of the roll and approximately 3 inches wide. Crimp the aluminum foil under the aluminum pie dish holding pie shell. Gently make a canopy over exposed pie crust. This will prevent the pie crust from browning and will give a nicer appearance to your pie.

Place pie in preheated 350 degree oven and bake for 55-60 minutes. Check middle of pie with a toothpick. If the toothpick pulls out clean, your pie is ready. If the toothpick has particles of batter on it, continue to bake pie checking every 1-2 minutes. Cooking times will vary depending upon your oven. Remove pie from oven and place on rack to rest and cool. Cut pie with wet knife. Total preparation and cooking time is approximately 1¼ hours.

BAKED APPLES WITH JACK DANIELS
AND BROWN SUGAR

At my childhood home we had a humungous apple tree in our backyard. If this tree was large I would have used that word – this tree was not large, it was humungous. It produced enough apples to supply the eastern seaboard and it was my job to pick up apples each morning and afternoon. Mother used these apples in fried apple pies, dumplings, homemade apple sauce, jams, jellies and we shared generously with the neighbors.

This apple tree on steroids also produced a plethora of switches. I was personally acquainted with more than a few. Because of its great height and the size of its limbs, this wonderful old tree also served as my best cover when I was under siege from neighborhood boys with tobacco stick broadswords.

In the mountains 50 miles to the north of my present home (Winston-Salem, North Carolina), apples are a money crop. When grouse hunting in our mountains it is a treat to find an old abandoned apple orchard. This treasure will generally hold a grouse or two and also produce a tasty treat that will quell your hunger and lighten your step. I concocted this recipe to showcase one of my favorite fruits – the apple. This dish can be served as a side dish and pairs well with any meal where one might use stewed apples. It goes exceptionally well with pheasant and quail. However, for this recipe the apples will wear their dessert hat.

8 cut, cored, quartered and unpeeled apples (Red Delicious, Rome or McIntosh apples are recommended)

1¾ sticks salted butter

½ cup Jack Daniels black label whiskey (to taste)

3¾ cups brown sugar lightly packed

1 cup white sugar

½ cup water

¼ teaspoon ground cinnamon

In a 15 inch by 10 inch by 2 inch baking dish place quartered, cut and cored apples skin side up 2 layers deep and add water. Place additional apple pieces over the holes created by the first layer until you have a relatively even surface (enough to fill dish to ¾ full). Cut butter into ¼ inch pats and place over apples. Drizzle whiskey over apples. Next pat brown sugar firmly over apples and cover brown sugar with white sugar. Do not pat. Simply smooth white sugar over brown sugar by hand. Sprinkle ground cinnamon lightly on top of white sugar. Preheat oven to 350 degrees. Place baking dish on baking tray or cookie sheet in case apples bubble over the baking dish. Bake at 350 degrees for 1 hour.

Place 1 or 2 apple pieces in a dessert bowl and pour a tablespoon of the apple juices over the apple slices. Top with a tablespoon of sea salt toasted English walnut pieces and finish with a dollop of whipped cream. This dessert can also be served with walnut pieces and a scoop of cinnamon ice cream (see *Tips for Cooking* section of this book for an easy recipe) for an equally tasty treat. Enjoy.

Total preparation and cooking time is approximately 1⅓ hours.

I rarely see it anymore but when I was a child, seafoam candy was one of the treats made by a number of the women in the Hicks' family. These delicious morsels were about the size of half a golf ball with a pecan half on top. It was my job to assist in cracking out the pecans in a manner that produced whole pecan halves without blemishing the meat.

I spent many evenings sitting on the floor with a little black iron hammer and a brick trying to master the task of cracking out pecans without smashing them. I finally acquired adequate skills at this feat and was able to produce whole pecan pieces almost every time. Today one can simply go to the store and buy them – not nearly as much fun.

In the South seafoam candy was generally made at Christmas time and gifted to special friends, layered on wax paper and contained in fruit-cake tins from the previous year. It was always appreciated by the recipient because it said the giver thought enough to take the time to make them a special treat. And special it was. Seafoam candy is a Southern confectionary delight. It is light, sweet and soft with just enough outer shell and pecan to give it a hint of crunch. It will literally melt in your mouth.

When you wish to say "Thank you" "I love you" or "Have a great day," this Old South cerci says it all.

2½ cups light brown sugar (packed)
¾ cup water
⅛ teaspoon salt
2 egg whites
1 pinch spoon cream of tarter
1 teaspoon vanilla
45 pecan halves

Combine first 3 ingredients in a 2 quart sauce pan, place on cold stove eye and set stove to medium-low heat (on my electric stove this is number 4). Cook mixture stirring occasionally. The mixture should cook at a simmer or bubble but not a hard boil. Cook your mixture until it cooks down to a point that it will spin a thread. A thread is an approximately 2 inch thin thread of syrup when the syrup is gently poured from the edge of a spoon. The total cooking time takes approximately 45 minutes. The last 5 minutes are critical and the mixture should be checked every 10-15 seconds. Before the mixture has cooked 30 minutes, beat egg whites with electric mixer with whisk attachment. When whites begin to stiffen, add cream of tartar and continue to mix until whites form stiff peaks. Change electric mixer to regular beating attachments and have vanilla ready to be added to water and sugar mixture.

Cover a cookie sheet with wax paper.

When the water and sugar mixture forms a thread, immediately remove from heat. Slowly pour hot sugar mixture over egg whites while continuing to beat egg whites with electric mixer at high speed. Add vanilla to your mixture and continue to beat until candy will hold its shape. This is when you can form it with your thumb and forefinger into a pecan-sized shape on a tablespoon. This requires approximately 8-9 minutes beating of your candy mixture. Do not over-beat as the mixture will harden as you form your candy pieces.

Spoon candy onto wax paper with a teaspoon, pushing candy from teaspoon with forefinger. Place candy pieces approximately 1 inch apart allowing for expansion. Candy will have little peaks and this is fine. Do not try to form candy into uniform pieces. Top each piece with a pecan half and mash gently. This will expand candy into pieces about ¾ to 1 inch thick and roughly the size of a golf ball in diameter. Allow candy to cool for about 30 minutes. Store candy on wax paper, seated on a plate in a cake box for best results Total preparation time is approximately 1½ hours. Makes approximately 45 pieces of the best candy you have ever tasted. Enjoy and share with someone special.

One of my all time favorite desserts was the chocolate pie made by my maternal grandmother Cora Hicks (known to me as Mama Hicks). Mama Hicks' chocolate pie consisted of a made-from-scratch pie shell, a chocolate fudge brownie type filling and a beautiful meringue topping cooked to perfection with amber droplets appearing on the peaks. It sounds pretty simple. And I guess if anyone including Mama Hicks had bothered to write down what she was doing in the kitchen, it would be. But no one wrote it down.

After Mama Hicks' death any number of Hicks' women, including my mother, attempted to make this pie. They were all good enough cooks and their efforts were tasty but no one successfully made the pie.

I remember as a four year old standing on a stool and watching Mama Hicks make this wonderful concoction. About all I could recall is that she melted hunks of chocolate in a make shift double boiler and had a sauce pan partially filled with water on another stove eye. I recall her dipping the chocolate as she stirred until it dripped in a form that pleased her. She then dripped a large droplet of chocolate in the pan of water. She allowed the chocolate to form a ball and then she carefully dipped it out with her fingers and rolled it between her thumb and first two fingers until it "felt right." When the chocolate ball rolled to please her, this dark, rich, brownie fudge wonderment was poured into a pie shell and baked until the time to add the meringue.

I was determined that this wonderful dessert was not going to pass from my family's life. With the help of a friend I was able to obtain some old chocolate pie recipes, parts of which were combined to form the baseline for the filling for this recipe. I have tweaked the recipe a number of times and added meringue. An abundance of humility and a smidgen of political correctness is all that prevents me from saying that I have captured Mama Hicks' chocolate pie recipe and maybe raised it a click. This recipe, in my opinion, is one of the best chocolate pies I have ever tasted. I hope you will come to share the same feelings. Make yourself a good pot of rich dark coffee and enjoy!

One 9 inch deep dish frozen pie shell (thawed)
¼ pound salted butter
2 squares unsweetened chocolate
2 whole eggs
3 egg whites
1¼ cups sugar
¼ cup flour
¼ teaspoon salt
1 teaspoon vanilla
½ teaspoon cream of tarter

Squeeze the dough around the edge of your pie shell between your thumb and forefinger and pinch scallops so your pie shell will look like a homemade pie shell and not a commercial product. Set pie shell aside.

Place butter and chocolate in a medium mixing bowl and microwave for approximately 3 minutes until the butter and the chocolate are melted. Fold butter and chocolate. In a large mixing bowl combine 2 eggs and 1 cup sugar and blend well with a whisk. Add your chocolate butter mixture to your eggs and blend. Add vanilla, flour and salt to mixture and continue blending. When mixture is well blended, pour the mixture into your unbaked and thawed pie shell. Cut strips of aluminum foil the width of the roll and approximately 3 inches wide. Crimp the aluminum foil under the aluminum pie dish holding your pie shell. Gently make a canopy over exposed pie crust. This will prevent the pie crust from browning and will give a nicer appearance to your pie.

Bake pie in a preheated oven at 350 degrees for approximately 40-43 minutes. About 30 minutes after you have placed the pie in the oven, make your meringue. Place egg whites in mixing bowl. With an electric mixer and whisk attachment, whip egg whites adding sugar as you whisk and continue to whisk until mixture forms stiff peaks. Add cream of tarter to promote stiffening of meringue as you mix. Whisk the meringue until you have good peaks when you pull the whisk from the meringue. Do not over-whisk the meringue. Making the meringue should take approximately 5 minutes.

When your pie has cooked for approximately 43 minutes, remove from the oven (do not turn oven off) and spread meringue fairly evenly over the top of the pie. Be sure to push the meringue to the pie shell so that it bonds and will not shrink and leave a space between the shell and the meringue. You may wish to have more meringue in the center of the pie sloping downwardly to the edges for effect. Make pretty twirls with your rubber spatula and pull it upwardly as you twirl to create peaks. Replace your pie in oven which has remained heated and cook for approximately 5-6 more minutes or until your meringue is a beautiful golden tan and you have lovely amber droplets on some of the peaks. Total cooking time for the pie and meringue should be approximately 49 minutes.

Remove pie from oven and place on rack to cool. Cut pie with a wet sharp knife cleaned after each slice to reduce drag.

Total preparation time is approximately 1 hour.

PECAN TASSIES

*F*rom the time of the earliest record keeping in the South, Southern squirrels and Southern cooks have made the pecan their nut of choice. Southern squirrels choose pecans for their natural abundance and thin shell that permits easy access to a goodly amount of tawny colored, rich tasting meat with a minimal amount of effort to get it. Southern cooks probably chose them for the same reasons.

Pecans are grown in every state in the South, but the great state of Georgia probably makes the boldest claims regarding this Southern culinary favorite. For centuries pecans have been woven into recipes for Southern sticky buns, pancakes, pies, cakes, pralines and candy. Pecans are also used as condiments for salads, congealed molds and soups. Pecans may not be as big of a staple in the South as grits, but pecans give their corn-ground rivals a run for the money.

The barbecue joints/places of the South universally offer banana pudding and pecan pie as their desserts of choice. Many people think pecan pie is preceded by the word Southern and rightfully it should be. Southern pecan pie is as much a part of the South as fast horses, pretty women, mint juleps and "Dixie."

An itsy-bitsy, teeny-weenie baby pecan pie is called a pecan tassie. Pecan tassies have for decades graced the buffets and tables of Southern ladies when they entertain. These wonderful morsels convey the taste of a pecan pie in a light and airy manner. A pecan tassie is a heavenly taste of brown sugar and pecans spun into a sinfully rich filling encased with a buttery shell as light as cotton candy.

Serve this Old South treat to your friends and bask in the smiles and praise you will receive for your efforts.

8 ounces cream cheese
1 stick salted creamy butter
1 cup sifted all purpose flour
1 egg
¾ cup brown sugar
1 tablespoon soft butter (for filling)
1 teaspoon vanilla
1 pinch spoon salt
1¼ cups coarsely chopped pecans
¼ tablespoon sea salt

Let cream cheese and stick of butter soften until easily depressed with a fork and blend together. Cream cheese and butter can be allowed to soften by sitting at room temperature or you can speed the process in a microwave by heating in 3-4 ten second intervals, turning butter and cream cheese at every interval. Watch carefully and do not over-heat or melt. Add flour and stir with a fork until well blended. Chill about 1 hour. Grease a mini muffin pan with shortening and dust with flour or use Pam for Baking brand cooking spray containing flour. Pour a cup of flour onto a dinner plate and place onto a towel that has been spread on the counter. Place the palms of both of your hands in the flour on the dinner plate so the dough will not stick to your palms. Remove dough from mixing bowl with a teaspoon approximately half a medium teaspoon at a time. Roll the dough in between palms into approximately 1 inch balls and place a ball in the center of each muffin cup in cooking tin. When all cups are filled, pour some flour into a measuring cup or coffee cup. Insert index finger into the flour and then press your finger into the center of each dough ball. Form the dough into cups so that the bottom and sides are pretty much the same thickness (about ¼ inch). You will need to flour your finger continuously to enable you to form the dough. After completing this you are ready for the filling.

Place pecan pieces in medium-sized frying pan over medium heat with sea salt. Toast pecan pieces for several minutes, turning often so as not to overcook. Remove pecan pieces with slotted spoon to a small bowl.

Combine egg, remaining 1 tablespoon soft butter, salt, sugar and vanilla and beat until creamy. Sprinkle 3 or 4 pecan pieces in the bottom of each pastry cup. Carefully place 1 teaspoon of filling onto pecan pieces. Place another 3 or 4 pecan pieces on top of filling. Bake in 325 degree oven for approximately 23-25 minutes or until filling is set. Let tassies cool for approximately 10-15 minutes before removing from pans. Tassies may be slightly sticky in the baking tin. Simply work the point of a paring knife gently between your tassie cup and the baking tin, apply slight pressure and the tassie will come free without breaking the crust. Keep tassies covered in cake box to maintain freshness. Makes 36 tassies.

Total preparation time is approximately 1 hour excluding chilling and resting time for dough.

Tips, Measurements and Preferences

*I*n this book I have used the terms "buzz" and "blend." By the term "buzz" I mean quick pulsating buzzes that achieve the desired consistency. This is particularly applicable when using a small food processor to chop nuts, jalapeños, etc. By the term "blend" I am using the chopping blade of the food processor to blend and chop. At no time during the blending process do I use a blending attachment. The chopping blade on a large food processor will both chop and blend when you are blending cheeses and the more moist ingredients, i.e. mayonnaise, sour cream, yogurt, whipped cream, etc. for your dips. Mash the button and hold for 15 seconds and check your consistency. I suggest taking a fork and pulling back some of the cheese ingredients to allow mayonnaise, sour cream, yogurt, whipped cream, etc. to be at the bottom so the chopping process does not make a cheese ball. After each 15 seconds, stop and check to see if you need to move more of the ingredients about in the food processor. Thirty to 45 seconds total time should give you the desired consistency. Generally when you make the base for the dip (grated cheese, cream cheese, etc.) you want a smooth creamy dip consistency that will hold on a cracker or rigid chip. If the dip mixture is a bit thick or dry after chopping/blending, add a tablespoon of mayonnaise, sour cream, yogurt or whipped cream (whichever is being used as the softener in the recipe). Blend/chop for five to ten seconds and check again.

To cook country ham for the recipes in this book, place ham in frying pan (seasoned cast iron skillets are great), cover the surface of pan with water (approximately 1/16 inch) and cook over medium heat. The water will cook out and the ham will brown a bit. Add a little more water and turn ham. Repeat. If ham is processed, follow cooking directions on package for cooking time. Do not overcook. Precooked processed ham takes only a couple of minutes for each side. Remove ham to a platter covered with paper towels. Blot ham well before cutting into pieces for recipes in this book.

The following is a quick way to transform a new cast iron frying pan into an heirloom black iron skillet. First scrub the inside of the pan with a steel wool pad containing soap and then wash the pan with regular dishwashing detergent, rinsing with hot water. Dry the pan and spread vegetable oil or shortening on the inside bottom and sides. If the pan has a lid, treat the inside of the lid in the same manner. Bake the seasoned pan and lid at low heat (approximately 200 degrees) for a half hour. Remove pan and lid from oven with hot mitts or glove and wipe down with paper towels. Return pan and lid to oven and bake for approximately two more hours. Remove pan and lid, cool pan and lid and return pan and lid to oven to bake for another two hours. Repeat this cool and bake process several times. After the pan and lid are seasoned, clean after each use with a soft scouring pad and hot water. Do not use soaps or detergents. Never ever put your seasoned pan or lid in a dishwasher for cleaning. After each use when you have cleaned the pan and lid, dry thoroughly, apply a film of vegetable oil, blot with paper towels and let dry before storing. If you are going to use your seasoned pan outdoors over an open flame, I suggest that you rub the outside of the pan with bar soap before using. This will greatly aid in clean up after a meal. The same process can be used for coffee pots and other metal cooking utensils when camping. Fine gray ashes from your fire and water can be used to clean your pan. Rinse thoroughly, boil clean hot water, dry and re-season for next use.

To hard boil eggs I simply place eggs on their side in a single layer in a sauce pan and cover the eggs with water by approximately 1/2 inch. Do not stand the eggs on end to gain more space. To do so will cause the yoke to droop to the bottom end of the egg and your cup will not be centered if you slice your eggs lengthwise. Bring water to a boil, cover, reduce heat to medium and cook for approximately 12 minutes. Drain hot water from sauce pan and replace with cold tap water. Let eggs rest for a minute or so until they are cool enough to handle. Crack egg gently on edge of sauce pan and peel carefully under cold running tap water. I start my peel at the large end of the egg. Once you have broken the membrane you can slide the membrane and shell easily with your thumb, turning the egg from the smaller end with your other hand.

For a slightly sweeter dip or spread, I prefer Dukes brand mayonnaise as it is made sweeter and produces a sweeter flavor.

Use real butter in all recipes in this book. When soft it spreads better than margarine or low fat spreads. It is my favorite in all baking recipes because it does not contain as much water as other products and it tastes great.

Use fresh herbs and spices as often as possible. Label the canned and jarred herbs and spices with the purchase date. Purge the spice rack every six months. Give your older spices to a soup kitchen and get a receipt for a tax deduction where applicable. You undermine your creative efforts if you don't use fresh herbs and spices.

If you do not have a food processor, grate cheese with a box grater. Other products may be finely chopped with a chef's knife and cutting board. Cuisinart is the food processor used for all recipes in this book. I grated the cheese with the grater attachment and then changed attachments to the chopping blade for chopping/blending.

Dips will become thicker with refrigeration. If dips are going to be refrigerated and used another day, storing in tightly sealed glass containers is best or a good plastic product like Tupperware. On the day you are going to serve dips, let the dips reach room temperature. If they are difficult to spread, you may need to add a tablespoon of mayonnaise, sour cream, yogurt or whipped cream (whichever is called for in the recipe) to soften to an easily spreadable consistency.

Peel and devein shrimp before cooking to avoid shellfish odor in kitchen. It is the shrimp shell, not the meat that gives off the cooking odor. Drop peeled, deveined and tailed shrimp into boiling water containing a half teaspoon of sea salt. Cook for approximately three minutes until pink. Do not overcook. Remove from heat immediately, drain, cover with cold water, drain again and place in large mixing bowl to rest. Cover in airtight container and refrigerate if not to be used at that time.

Chop spring onions on a chopping board with a chef's knife. Do not use a food processor as it will bruise the onions.

Buy your blackberries from the market unless you are particularly fond of pain. See story.

When purchasing cantaloupes smell the depression where the vine was attached. If it has a good cantaloupe smell, the rind looks good and pebbly, it thumps solid and does not have soft spots – you probably have a good melon.

For some reason figs generally taste sweeter when the end where the fig was attached to the bush or tree is broken off instead of cut.

Use excess key limes for gin and tonics. A cut key lime can be sprinkled with Fruit Fresh produce protector and wrapped in plastic food wrap. Limes will keep nicely in refrigerator for several days.

Small sweet potatoes cooked in the jacket, peeled from the top like a banana and a small chip of warm butter make a tasty and healthy treat.

Making your real pumpkin jack-o-lantern into pies provides not only fun, but a feast as well.

To make Jim's Joe, place a one inch piece of Heath Bar in the bottom of an Irish whiskey mug and pour approximately half full of freshly perked coffee of choice. Then add a tablespoon of Bailey's Original Irish Cream liqueur, a tablespoon of Kahlúa liqueur and a tablespoon of Arrow Creme de Cacao dark liqueur. Place coffee in microwave for approximately 20 seconds to reheat after adding liqueurs. Top with whipped cream, sprinkle with Frangelico liqueur and shaved Heath Bar or shaved sweet chocolate for a wonderful drink.

To make a good legal homemade brandy, peel three or four white mountain peaches and place in a quart mason jar. Fill the jar with Jacques Cardin Napoleon Brandy, cap and let rest for several months. Nectar for the gods.

To separate egg whites from yolks, with clean hands break the egg and let the white of the egg drip through your fingers into a mixing bowl retaining the yolk on your fingers. Place the yolk aside in a bowl to be used in another recipe.

After you have thawed your frozen pie shell, squeeze the dough around the edge of the pie shell between thumb and forefinger and pinch scallops so your pie shell will look like a homemade pie shell and not a commercial product.

To give a nicer appearance to your pie and prevent exposed pie crust from browning too much, cut strips of aluminum foil the width of the roll and approximately 3 inches wide. Crimp the aluminum foil under the aluminum pie dish holding your pie shell. Gently make a canopy over your exposed pie crust, fill pie shell and bake.

To make cake layers more moist, punch rows of holes approximately an inch apart with a dinner fork and gently drizzle about three tablespoons of coconut milk, pineapple juice or orange juice over your layer. Your choice of drizzle will depend upon what you deem will taste best with the icing to be used on cake.

If you are using boxed cake mix instead of from-scratch cake layer recipe, simply substitute milk for water in recipe and your layers will come out more moist.

Prior to greasing and dusting cake pans, place the cake pan on wax paper over a cutting board or marble candy/cookie slate. With a sharp knife, scissor point or razor blade, cut around the cake pan. After you have your wax paper bottom liner, grease the inside bottom and sides of the cake pan with shortening. Place the wax paper liner on inside bottom of pan and grease wax paper. Then put several tablespoons of all purpose flour in cake pan and shake it around until the bottom and sides are lightly dusted. Dump excess flour in trash.

I prefer to dust cake pans that will be used for chocolate layers with coco powder instead of white flour.

When greasing a cake pan with shortening, you can use a sandwich bag as a glove or rubber latex serving gloves to avoid messy hands.

Pam for Baking brand cooking spray (contains flour) may be used as a substitute for shortening when greasing cake pans and for dusting pans with flour. The layers baked in the test kitchen using this product pulled away from the pan on the sides nicely enough but the bottom of the layers had a tendency to slightly stick in the middle of the cake pan. Allow layers to cool and run a paring knife around the edge of pan to be sure that your layer and pan are separated. Then using a round blade dinner knife, gently go under the edge of the cake and slightly lift the cake enough to insert your fingers. Then lightly lift until the cake loosens from the pan in the middle. This was done without a great deal of effort and the layers turned out fine.

When making cake layers from a boxed cake mix, pour the contents of the box into a large mixing bowl and gently whisk the flour to avoid any lumps. Pour wet ingredients into a different mixing bowl. Beat eggs, vegetable oil, warm butter, etc. until well blended. Thirty seconds to a minute should do this. With your hand make a nest in the center of flour to receive wet ingredients. Pour wet ingredients into nest. Mix ingredients with an electric mixer until blended. About two minutes should do this. Pour batter into the center of prepped cake pan.

After placing raw cake batter in cake pan, move the batter to the edges with a rubber spatula so that you do not have more batter in the center. Hold the sides of the pan and bump the pan flat on kitchen counter three or four times to seat the batter evenly and help prevent doming of the layers.

If cake layers have domes, use a long blade bread knife and cut horizontally across the layer to remove only the dome. A cheese wire, dental floss or clean monofilament fishing line will do the job if you do not have a long blade bread knife.

Cake layers may be made in advance of your party and frozen in airtight freezer bags for up to 30 days. On the day of your party simply remove the frozen layers from the freezer bags and allow layers to thaw completely on a plate before attempting to apply icing.

When icing a multi-layered cake, you can hold the layers in place with wooden skewers until icing process is complete. Then remove skewers and cover holes on top layer with icing.

If homemade caramel icing becomes too thick to spread, add a tablespoon of half & half milk and place back over heat for approximately one minute, stirring until icing achieves a spreading consistency.

Commercial cinnamon ice cream is often difficult to find. You can make homemade cinnamon ice cream by softening vanilla ice cream and adding ground cinnamon and then refreezing to original firmness. The general rule of thumb is one teaspoon ground cinnamon per pint of ice cream.

Place iced cakes in a closed cake box. Do not refrigerate baked cake unless required to do so because of fresh fruit garnishment, whipped cream, etc. Refrigeration will make cake sweat.

Homemade candies should also be kept in a cake box or tin. Exposure to air will cause candy pieces to harden at an accelerated rate.

MEASUREMENTS

Measurement Conversions

1 pinch	=	less than 1/8 tsp.
1 Tbsp.	=	3 tsp.
2 Tbsp.	=	1 oz.
4 Tbsp.	=	1/4 cup
5 Tbsp. + 1 tsp.	=	1/3 cup
8 Tbsp.	=	1/2 cup
10 Tbsp. + 2 tsp.	=	2/3 cup
12 Tbsp.	=	3/4 cup
16 Tbsp.	=	1 cup

1 cup	=	8 oz.
1 pint	=	16 oz.
1 quart	=	32 oz.
1 gallon	=	128 oz.

1 cup	=	1/2 pint
2 cups	=	1 pint
4 cups	=	1 quart
2 pints	=	1 quart
4 pints	=	1/2 gallon
8 pints	=	1 gallon
4 quarts	=	1 gallon

TEST KITCHEN BRAND PREFERENCES

Almonds – Planters

Artichoke Hearts – Haddon House

Baby Clams – Orleans

Bacon Pieces – Oscar Meyer Real Bacon Recipe

Baking Soda – Rumford

Bartlett Pears – Del Monte Orchard Select

Bing Cherries – Melissa's

Black Eyed Peas – Bush's

Black Olive Tapenade – H.T. Traders

Blackberry Preserves – H.T. Traders

Blue Cheese – Treasure Cave

Blueberry Preserves – Bonne Maman

Brown Sugar – Dixie Crystal

Butter – Land O' Lakes

Cake Mixes – Duncan Hines

Cashew Nuts – Planters

Champagne – Korbel

Chocolate Covered Espresso Beans – Fresh Market

Cling Peaches – Del Monte Orchard Select

Coconut Milk – Coco Goya

Coffee – Millstone

Condensed Milk – Eagle

Cooking Spray – Pam Butter Flavor

Corn Syrup – Karo Light Corn Syrup

Country Ham – Saddler

Cream Cheese – Kraft Original Philadelphia

Cream of Coconut – Goya

Cream of Tartar – McCormick

Creole Seasoning – Tony Chacheres

Dried Apricots – Hines Nut Co.

Flour – Red Band or Lily White

Frozen Pie Shell – (your choice)

Fruit Fresh Produce Protector

Goat Cheese – Ile de France

Graham Crackers – Keebler

Green Olives Stuffed with Pimentos – Mario

Half & Half – (your choice)

Hazelnuts – Planters

Honey – Naturally Healthy Pure Raw

Jalapeño Peppers (jarred) – Louisiana or Mt. Olive

Light Corn Syrup – Karo

Lime Curd – Dickensons

Macadamia Nuts – Planters

Marshmallow Cream – Kraft Jet Puffed

Mayonnaise – Dukes

Montague Cheese – (your choice)

Monterey Jack Cheese – Kraft

Orange Juice – Minute Maid

Parmesan Cheese – DiGiorno

Peanuts – Planters

Pecans – Planters

Pepperjack Cheese – Kraft

Pepperoni – Sara Lee

Pickled Eggs – Hiatt

Pimento Pieces (jarred) – Dromedary

Pineapple Juice – Del Monte

Pine Nuts – Melissa's

Pistachio Nuts – Sunkist

Plum Preserves – Bonne Maman Damson

Raisins – Sun Maid

Red Raspberry Spread – St. Dalfour

Roasted Red Peppers (jarred) – Cento

Sea Salt – Baleine

Shortening – Crisco All Vegetable

Smoked Oysters – Orleans

Sour Cream – Daisy

Stilton Cheese – Crest Royal Blue

Strawberry Preserves – Smuckers

Sun Dried Figs – Sun Maid

Sun Dried Tomatoes – Melissa's

Sweet Orange Marmalade – Smuckers

Sweet Pickle Cubes – Mt. Olive

Unsweetened Chocolate – Bakers

Vanilla – McCormick

Vegetable Oil – Crisco

Walnuts – Planters

Water Crackers – Carr's

Whipped Cream – Cool Whip

White Cheddar Cheese – Kraft Vermont

White Chocolate Morsels – Nestle

White Sugar – Dixie Crystal

Worcestershire Sauce – Lea & Perrins

Yellow Cheddar Cheese – Kraft Cracker Barrel

Yellow Mustard – French's

NOTES

NOTES